Euripides
Plays: One

Medea, The Phoenici...

As Athens sank deeper into ... couldn't win, Euripides challe... In each of these three plays he portrayed individuals so incensed by injustice and grown so murderous in pursuit of redress that their actions can only destroy their families and spawn greater evil. *Medea*, *The Phoenician Women* and *The Bacchae* are presented here in new translations, accurate, scholarly and tested in production, with an introduction by J. Michael Walton.

Euripides was born near Athens between 485 and 480 BC and grew up during the years of Athenian recovery after the Persian Wars. His first play was presented in 455 BC but he failed to win the first prize for tragedy until 441 and rarely afterwards. Despite this, nineteen of his plays survive, including *Electra*, *Hippolytus*, *Ion* and *The Trojan Women*, a greater number than those of Aeschylus and Sophocles combined. His later plays are marked by a sense of disillusion at the futility of human aspiration which amounts on occasion to a philosophy of absurdism. A year or two before his death he left Athens to live at the court of Archelaus of Macedon where he died in 406 BC.

The front cover shows 'Woman Crying' by Pablo Picasso © DACS 1987.

EURIPIDES

Plays: One
Introduced by J. Michael Walton

Medea
translated by Jeremy Brooks

The Phoenician Women
translated by David Thompson

The Bacchae
translated by J. Michael Walton

Methuen Drama

METHUEN WORLD CLASSICS

These translations first published in Great Britain
as a Methuen paperback original in 1988 by Methuen London Ltd.
Reprinted in 1992 by Methuen Drama
an imprint of Reed Consumer Books Ltd
Michelin House, 81 Fulham Road, London SW3 6RB
and Auckland, Melbourne, Singapore and Toronto
and distributed in the United States of America
by Heinemann, a division of Reed Publishing (USA) Inc.,
361 Hanover Street, Portsmouth, New Hampshire NH 03801 3959
Reissued with a new cover design 1994
Reprinted 1994

Medea translation copyright © Jeremy Brooks 1988
The Phoenician Women translation copyright © David Thompson 1988
The Bacchae translation copyright © J. Michael Walton 1988
This collection and introduction
copyright © Methuen London Ltd. 1988

British Library Cataloging in Publication Data

Euripides
    Euripides: Plays One.
I. Title II. Euripides. Medea
III. Euripides. The Phoenician women
IV. Euripides The Bacchae V. Selections, *English*
881'.01   PA3975.A2

ISBN 0-412-17550-2

Photoset in Plantin by 🅰 Tek Art Limited, Croydon, Surrey
Printed and bound in Great Britain by
Cox & Wyman Ltd, Reading, Berkshire

CAUTION

5.99

CONTENTS

INTRODUCTION

There are two reasons for studying the history of the theatre. One is historical, the other theatrical. The plays of any period and the theatre for which they were written offer a special insight into the nature of a civilisation, its ideas and its preoccupations. Were it not so, drama could make no claim to being an independent discipline deserving study at the highest level. An individual play is something in addition. Once it was a performance piece. If it cannot talk to new generations of audience, it may as well stay on the shelf; no dishonourable place perhaps, but, for a play, the equivalent of being put out to grass in decent but ineffective retirement.

Greek tragedy spent the best part of two thousand years confined to the ivory tower with only the most sporadic of forays into the marketplace. The last hundred years have seen these forays become regular, though hardly routine; but seldom has the state of the theatre, nor the state of the world, seemed more opportune for a reappraisal of the theatre of the Greeks. And of all Greek plays, none seem so modern as those of Euripides.

The Athenian theatre derived its form and its impetus from the special circumstances under which it operated. The plays are powerful pieces. They can speak for themselves. But an informed account of the background to their first performance must throw light on the dramatic method and iron out some of those factors which for so long made Greek tragedy appear inaccessible to the ordinary playgoer. This is especially true of Euripides, much of whose work served as a challenge to what the audiences of his own time had come to expect.

In the spring of 431 BC Euripides' *Medea* was produced at the Great Dionysia in Athens. As was customary, each of three tragedians presented four plays in competition. None of the other eleven plays has survived, but the record shows that the group which included *Medea* was placed last. More than twenty years later – the date of *The Phoenician Women* is uncertain, though 409 BC seems likely – Euripides was more successful, coming second with the set from which his 'Theban' play has survived. *The Bacchae* was almost certainly produced in Athens in 405 BC. *Iphigeneia in Aulis,* from the same group, is also extant and this time Euripides was successful in winning first prize. This can hardly be regarded as a consolation for previous disappointment, as he had already been dead for over a year. The posthumous *The Bacchae* was not the playwright's only victory in the dramatic competitions. He had four 'firsts' to his name while alive, but four seems niggardly in a working life of fifty years.

Only two months after *Medea* in 431 BC, Attica was invaded by Archidamus, King of Sparta, and the Peloponnesian War between Athens and Sparta began in earnest. It was to last intermittently for twenty-seven years and end with total defeat for the Athenians the year after *The Bacchae*. These two plays serve as a frame for a war which demolished Athens' empire and almost her civilisation. *The Phoenician Women* was in the thick of it, between a civil war in Athens itself and Euripides' departure into self-imposed exile in Macedon, where he spent his last years at the court of King Archelaus.

So varied are the plays that have come down to us that generalisations about Greek tragedy or comedy are almost always misleading. What does seem unarguable is that the function of the playwright in society was accepted by the Athenians as a didactic one and that if Euripides was unable regularly to commend himself to the festival juries it was largely because his message was too disturbing for these war-torn years. Times of hostilities are in most civilisations the least productive of periods for serious drama. Despite this, and despite reservations at the time about Euripides' work, in Athens of the fifth century BC war seems to have served as a positive stimulus.

The work of four major Athenian playwrights survives, discounting the meagre helping of Menander's new comedy written a century after the death of Euripides. Aeschylus died in 456 BC, having lived and worked through the defeat of the Persians at the battles of Marathon and Salamis and the sometimes painful birth of the new democracy. Seven of his plays survive, the same number as of Sophocles, born thirty years after Aeschylus, who grew up to defeat him in competition and outlive even Euripides. Nineteen plays are attached to Euripides' name. One is a dubious attribution; another not a tragedy, but a satyr play performed as a comic afterpiece to three tragedies. The surviving tragedies of this 'unpopular' playwright still outnumber those of Aeschylus and Sophocles combined. Aristophanes, the supreme comic writer of the fifth century, whose 'old comedies' represent a genre in their own right, was barely fourteen when the Peloponnesian War began, and all but two of his surviving eleven comedies were played before the defeat by Sparta.

The curious conclusion from all this data is that of the forty-four plays which comprise the corpus of classical drama, the seven of Aeschylus date from the early part of the fifth century BC. Of the remaining thirty-seven, more than thirty have the Peloponnesian War as a back drop. In few of these is war seen as anything but hateful. In tragedies such as the *Hecuba* or *The Trojan Women* of Euripides, the degrading effects on victor and vanquished alike could only have been seen as a comment on the behaviour of the Athenians, no less than the Spartans, during the current hostilities. Sophocles is less outspoken, but Aristophanes weighs in with absurdist visions of the God of War pounding the Greek states in his mortar in *Peace* and of bellicose Athenian and Spartan males reduced through sexual deprivation to rampant pacifism in *Lysistrata*. Through year after year of campaigns and battles, major writers risked accusations of defeatism, treachery even, by persisting in questioning the conduct of a war which every year Athens looked less likely to win.

But if the war could never be eliminated from the sensibilities of his audience, or the audience of any other playwright of the time, Euripides pointed to other truths about the human condition which were so unpalatable that it was not until after his death that audiences were prepared to stomach them. Not all his plays are about war widows and the pointless waste of young life decked out as martyrdom. He wrote of the power of the passions, the arbitrariness of fate and the ambiguity of motive. So did Aeschylus and Sophocles, but Euripides did more. He debunked reputations, mortal and divine. He pinpointed hypocrisy and exposed its disguises. Medea murders her children, but she is driven to the act by male callousness. The combined efforts of the entire family of Oedipus cannot prevent his two sons killing one another and dragging the whole world into their mutual loathing. Pentheus is dismembered by his mother, both of them victims of a life force they have tried to deny. Passion is irresistible. The internal war for Euripides was as mad and destructive as the external.

All the Greek tragedians are absorbed by strength and weakness. Euripides matches the others in this, but in this world strength and weakness are deceptive, human characters more circular than polarised. His weapon is surprise. Nothing appears to him to be more fun than leading an audience down the path of his moral garden and then up-ending them on to the compost heap. Heroines prove tartars, sinners find a bit of halo to polish. His paradoxes can be as bizarre as those of Aristophanes, as thought-provoking as those of Brecht.

The greatest paradox of all is that Euripides should have been creating his subtle dishes from a recipe whose ingredients at first sight appear so unpromising. The physical conditions that dictated the nature of the Greek theatre seem appropriate to the powerful theatrical stroke and the unequivocal statement, but hardly to the nuances of sub-text. Perhaps this was another reason for the shock with which audiences reacted. But one thing is sure. Euripides knew precisely what he was doing, and dramatic effects, including those identified by critics centuries later, can with some confidence be ascribed to the playwright's design. This is not to suggest that he could or would have subscribed to all the theories propounded about his plays, still less claimed paternity to the wilder aberrations perpetrated by some modern directors. It does mean that he created drama which was ahead of its own time and better suited than that of his contemporaries to the twentieth-century mind.

The physical conditions that obtained in the Athenian theatre in the fifth century BC are open to dispute. This is both a blessing and a curse; a blessing because it continually licenses scholars to speculate and practitioners to create; a curse because the temptation for both to disregard the perspective of the other has resulted in the relegation of the classical repertoire to the lower divisions, with only the occasional cup-run to stimulate season-ticket holders. If such a sporting metaphor appears strained, let it be defended by reference to the sense of occasion which overlaid the whole process of play production in classical Athens, with the same civic significance given to dramatic as to other festivals, including the athletic.

It is customary, and right, to draw special attention to the religious nature of Greek festival. The occasions devoted primarily to dramatic performance took place during the winter or early spring: the Lesser or Rural Dionysia in a variety of locations during December; the Lenaea, at which comedy was featured, in January; and the Great or City Dionysia in March or the beginning of April. This latter was the festival for which the plays of Aeschylus, Sophocles and Euripides were written, as well as some of the plays of Aristophanes. The Great Dionysia included processions and proclamations, sacrifices and ceremonies as well as the three sets of tragic plays and four or five old comedies, all in the space of at most six days. The god Dionysus presided, his statue escorted into the theatre as part of the opening ceremony and taken back to its shrine on the road to Eleutherae at the conclusion. Dionysus was always God of the Theatre from the first introduction of dramatic performance into the festival of the Great Dionysia, generally accepted as about 534–530 BC. By this time the festival, inaugurated by Peisistratus some twenty-five years earlier, was well established, though the Dionysiac religion had not made an appearance in mainland Greece until fairly late, later certainly than the twelve Olympians who form the Greek pantheon and periodically interfere with the mortal world in *The Iliad* and *The Odyssey*. Passages of these two epics of Homer were recited at the Great Dionysia both before and after the introduction of dramatic production.

Dating for any events in the pre-classical period is at best hazy, but the war against Troy provided a convenient hitching-post for myth. Most of the heroes could relate at least their genealogies to the ten-year siege by the Greeks seeking the return of Helen and the ten-year period after Troy's sack which it took Odysseus to reach his home in Ithaca. Historically this razing of Troy is believed to have occurred about 1200 BC. As Homer was probably not creating or compiling his poems until four hundred years later, and it was another three hundred years before anyone began to think of writing history, what is remarkable is not so much the contradictions as the fact that there should have been any kind of coherence at all.

The Greek tragedies did for the most part relate to a world that really had existed, though some of the more grotesque figures seem the progeny of nightmare rather than folk memory. *The Bacchae* probably does record the arrival in Northern Greece of an eastern deity whose properties were disruptive and hence opposed, but who eventually caused the destruction of the young King. Pentheus is the grandson of Cadmus, founder of Thebes. This is the same Cadmus whose great-great-grandson, by a more durable if hardly better-starred line, is Oedipus. Heracles, the best known of all Greek heroes, had a connection with Thebes through a marriage to Megara, daughter of Creon, the uncle/brother-in-law of Oedipus. Heracles provides a link, if peripherally, to both the Trojan War and the expedition of the Argonauts which resulted in Jason bringing Medea to Corinth. To compound confusion, it is Creon's daughter for whom Jason jilts Medea, but, as King of Corinth, he is a different Creon from the Creon who becomes King of Thebes. The Greek stage world does consist of a seeming pool of wandering characters – Theseus is another – who happen in from time to time, rather as though they were Pirandellian creations waiting for a cue to enter the play, any play.

When they lived and what they really were is not in itself discernible or important. What is important is that the world of myth was a confused and swirling one, not dissimilar to that of King Arthur, or even the Lear and Macbeth of the English and Scottish Dark Ages. As Shakespeare latched on to the names and gave them dramatic substance for the audience of Jacobean England, so Euripides enjoyed the freedom of ready-made figures, whose given qualities consisted less of fixed characteristics than of specific deeds. It was the circumstances surrounding them which were his raw material. Gods as well as humans were liable to find their motives questioned. Dionysus himself was not exempt at his own festival in his own theatre, and in front of his own statue.

Every aspect of the Greek dramatic festivals seems geared to creating an occasion when religious observance became fully integrated with civic ritual. The theatrical power generated fuelled both the individual and the corporate need. The ability of playwright and performer to rouse emotion was the means by which the audience assessed a play, but the occasion made the theatre doubly dangerous. On the one hand, the temper of the times was on display. On the other, the theatre was a place which seethed with new ideas. When characters were forced to face realities, so were the audience. If a general warning against excess was the message reduced to its simplest, it was a moral banged home with startling frankness.

Whether the ultimate aim was to exercise or exorcise the emotions so roused was all one to Plato, who would have none of it in the ideal state he proposed in his *Republic*. Plato shared with the Pentheus of *The Bacchae* an instinctive appreciation of the power of Dionysus. To puritans, both then and since, the theatre represents a threat. Its instinct is for the subversive. The more sensitive the times, the more alarming the frankness of a Euripides must seem.

An Athenian audience was large. The auditorium of the theatre for which Euripides wrote, as renovated by Pericles, must have held at least seventeen thousand. Today the amphitheatre at Verona might offer an audience a comparable experience, but even that resembles more the Greek theatre of the fourth century, when individual performance overshone content. Comparisons with modern pop concerts or football matches are actually misleading, and the evangelist meeting, where emotion smothers reason, offers no proper parallel to the promotion of rational argument through highly charged example, which is the mark of the Athenian drama. Only in the East might it be possible to find a tradition in which the world of the spirit still relates art to life, extolling the community it informs.

This is not to suggest that a modern audience has been disinherited from the Greek canon, only that there are pitfalls. Reconstruction of the original conditions of performance could never be more than an academic exercise with the single purpose of providing an insight into how and why playmakers of a past period made plays as they did. It may answer questions relating to stages and scenery, to costume and convention, to buildings and bank balances, actors and audiences. Some of these conditions may even be artificially recreated. Others cannot, notably the audience, whose expectations contribute enough to a performance to render the period replica vapid. No, the whole exercise revolves around the search that a modern director must undertake for equivalents which are properly rooted in the original material. If no precise analogue might seem to exist for a masked actor intoning strict verse to a musical accompaniment before a dancing Chorus and an audience of seventeen thousand ancient Athenians, then let the director look to essences and recall that the finest theatrical minds of the last hundred years have all seen the theatre as a synthesis of other art forms, overlaid with something that is unique to the theatre. Whether they did so consciously or not, Craig, Reinhardt, Meyerhold, Brecht, Artaud and Brook have all returned to the theatrical priorities of Aeschylus, Sophocles and Euripides.

All this is for the directors of these plays, and for the readers too, who should not be allowed to assume, because words are what have survived, that Euripides' art is a wholly literary one. The nature of the occasion was clearly one factor affecting the plays' form. Another was the physical aspect of the theatre and the way in which it related to a series of performance conventions. It was out of these conventions, which at first sight might appear to be at odds with his material, that Euripides was able to fashion his distinctive dramatic style. The earliest form of tragedy featured a chorus and a single actor. Whether this actor had ever been one of the chorus is less clear, but the choral element, that is dance and song, remained central to the whole performance throughout the classical period. Aristotle, in the *Poetics*, confirms an impression which the plays point to: that Aeschylus introduced a second actor, Sophocles a third. The chorus numbered twelve or fifteen for tragedy, twenty-four for comedy. These norms did not restrict the number of characters to two or three, of course, and a secondary chorus was used on occasions, as well as a large number of supernumeraries. But there was no regular fourth 'actor' and the Euripides plays which survive can comfortably be performed by a company of three speaking actors. It is possible that the received manuscripts include emendations geared to suit the touring system of the fourth and third centuries BC. Sorting out exactly what may or may not be original Euripides has been a critical exercise for centuries, but, as in the long run it boils down to scholarly preference, we would be advised to accept the authenticity of what we have, unless it simply fails to make sense. In addition to the three actors, *Medea* has parts for two children, who appear with their mother and later call for help off-stage. *The Phoenician Women* has a cast of eleven, apart from the Chorus, which is a lot to divide amongst three performers, but can be done. *The Bacchae* is straightforward enough, as long as one can accept the actor who plays Pentheus later returning as his own mother Agave, brandishing her son's head (or mask) on her Bacchic wand.

The question *why* the Greek playwrights should have restricted themselves to a limited number of actors is a different matter and has received a variety of answers. The more compelling relate to money. By Euripides' time, actors, though not chorus, were professionals and were allotted by the state to each playwright whose submission of plays had been accepted for festival production. Other expenses, with the exception of the theatre fabric managed on a commercial basis by the *architekton*, were the responsibility of an individual citizen, who had little choice about subsidising the state in this or some similar enterprise. This *choregos* equipped a production to certain standards. Paying for one or more extra actors, as seems to have been essential for some of the comedies at least, may well have been beyond the pocket or inclination of some sponsors, especially as they had to costume the entire production and pay a choreographer, perhaps also a director.

The Greek actor was not, as is now generally agreed, the grotesque figure of Hellenistic or Roman times. Those infamous 'high boots', so beloved of the compilers of potted histories of the theatre, are not of the fifth century BC at all, and every visual representation of the tragic mask from contemporary vase-painting suggests realism rather than exaggeration. The *cothurnus* was worn by the tragic actor, but it was a soft knee-length boot with no platform sole. By the time of Euripides, costume seems to have possessed some formal elements, depending on character, but was based on everyday dress of the time – the *chiton* or tunic which was pinned at the shoulder and a *peplos* or cloak where appropriate. Rank or profession could be signified by specialist costume, by colour or by what was carried. Many characters could be identified simply by appearance. Armour, a traveller's hat, winged sandals, a suppliant's offerings, lionskin and club, trident, thyrsus, mourning robes, old men's staffs – all conveyed meaning. Euripides was reputed to have first moved in the direction of realism with his portrayal of the beggar-king Telephus as more beggar than king, but the principal weapon of the actor puts this realism into perspective. That weapon was the mask and, however 'real' the mask, masked acting is not realistic.

The mask could vary in colour and in aspect – darker for a man, lighter for a woman. There were specialist masks for some of the grosser characters, or, for example, for the blinded Oedipus. In comedy there were portrait masks, but, natural or monstrous, the wearing of masks dictates a way of acting with which few modern performers are familiar or comfortable. Masked acting is a precise and definite means of translating speech into physical expression. The language of gesture, *cheironomia,* was the true language of the Greek theatre, serving to point and promote both speech and song. The extent to which the chorus danced mimetically can never be known, but the range of emotions they were called upon to portray and the scope of the actions they describe cannot but read to the theatre practitioner as choreographic instruction. Attempts have been made, if sporadically, to recreate this choreography from metrical pattern. The shared rhythm of certain lyric passages suggests that the principal actors too could at times be classified as much dancers as actors. With accompanying music from double pipe, possibly lute and percussion, all but lost, the total nature of Greek performance must remain conjectural. What the mask demands of the actor can be pinned down, if only because of the universality to be found among those theatre traditions, mainly oriental, in which the mask is still the centre of the performance. The voice was clearly important to the Greek actor – Sophocles reputedly gave up performing because his was too weak for a massive open-air theatre – and audiences were used to listening closely to argument in the Athenian Assembly. But to ignore the physical dimension of Greek performance is to defy the tradition from which acting sprang.

When it comes to the shape of the theatre and the settings used to identify location the waters are again murky. The Periclean theatre in Athens, that is the Theatre of Dionysus as it was modified in the second half of the fifth century BC, possessed a scenic background, or *skene*, which was wooden. This much is known with some certainty. A hundred years later it was replaced by the first stone facade. A wooden *skene* could imply no more than the most meagre of backings for the actor, with a place to enter from and exit to that did not involve the long walk right out of the theatre which the chorus had to use. The precinct offered an arena of three separate but interconnected spaces: the *skene* with an acting area in front; and the *theatron*, for spectators, with seats following two-thirds of the perimeter line of the third area, the *orchestra*, or dancing-place. For the most part the three groups – actors, audience, chorus – kept to their own place, with the actors playing in a shallow plane before the *skene*. The chorus did sometimes encroach on to this area and the actors clearly made the odd inroad into the *orchestra*, while all performers could use the *parodoi* between *theatron* and *skene* for entrance and exit.

Most Greek plays are set in front of a house or a palace, as are *Medea*, *The Phoenician Women* and *The Bacchae*. Others are not, a few requiring a change of location from scene to scene in the same play. Wooden stages unfortunately disappear without trace, and though vase paintings can again be helpful in sorting out theatrical conditions, those which may be inspired by dramatic scenes were never intended as 'production photographs'. The outstanding question is whether any additional stage-settings were employed. 'Actual locale and any variation from the stock exterior can be assumed from the spoken word,' runs one argument. 'On the contrary,' runs another, 'Sophocles is credited by Aristotle with inventing *skenographia*, and that can only mean "scene-painting".' Certainly there is solid evidence for the use by Euripides' time of the *ekkuklema*, a wheeled platform for the display of tableaux, and the *mechane*, or stage-crane, for the revelation of gods. These pieces of machinery did not add to a realistic effect – they would hardly have done that – but did extend the range of spatial and visual possibilities. The strongest advocate of the 'empty space' cannot deny that the Greek theatre was not simply a place of the imagination. The argument for individual design features – a raised stage, porch units, painted panels and properties at the very least – is hard to resist, but can never be taken as proved. It is perhaps not unfair to add that the greater the devotion of the critic to language and the spoken word, the less he or she seems to see a need for staging devices.

The strange and intriguing aspect of any such disputes is that the bare bones of Athenian stage practice are sufficiently clearly defined for solution to specific staging issues to prove largely irrelevant in identifying how Euripides manipulated audience expectation. The Greek theatre was at all times an artistic conglomerate rooted in artifice. Like other art forms it was built up in layers. These layers involved ways of seeing. They involved levels of understanding. This was a theatre of example and parable. Touching reality only at a tangent, it was at its most powerful and poignant when creating its own world from which the audience could draw their own conclusions. Tragedy may not have been invented by Aeschylus, but for us today he defined it, examining the plight of a Prometheus or an Orestes in grand, passionate terms. Sophocles brought man to the centre, man at the level of hero, however flawed: Ajax or Oedipus. Euripides received the myths from the past and his theatre from Aeschylus and Sophocles. What he could not do was reconcile the old stories with the human condition as he saw it. So with the framework of a heroic theatre, he took his heroic characters and made them behave like people. Sometimes they seem sadistic, sometimes comic, often truly pathetic. The audience were confronted with the theatre they knew – acting-areas, masks, chorus, everything they understood the theatre to be. The characters still spoke in verse, but what they talked about were no longer abstract ideas or the conflict of ideals. They sounded real, and that made people uncomfortable. Now in the twentieth century they still sound real and they still have something to say to us.

All they need is a means, but that ought not to prove a problem in a contemporary theatre, more aware than at any time in its history of the full range of modes of expression. The danger of promoting the form at the expense of the content is, of course, a real one, and for this reason, if for no other, Euripides deserves to be read in versions as close as possible to the received manuscripts. If some references seem at this range to be elusive or simply quaint, then that is to be expected, and any director is at liberty to adapt to suit the audience. What should and can shine through is the kind of blazing honesty about human beings and the world they live in that makes a nonsense of the 'barrier' of two and a half thousand years. The Athenians knew they needed their theatre. We should be in no doubt that our theatre needs Euripides.

Medea

What gift of the gods could be finer for man
Than to raise up his hand o'er the head of his foe,
Triumphant. *The Bacchae (l. 878–80)*

So sing the Chorus of Asian Bacchants relishing the prospect of Pentheus' humiliation and death for opposing the god Dionysus. A modern audience, holding, however notionally, to Christian ideals of charity and compassion, may wince when confronted by such a single-minded impulse to revenge. An Athenian one would have seen nothing wrong in retaliating for injury sustained, though the ensuing complications are at the heart of almost all tragic situations. Euripides was not the first of the Greek tragedians to use this apparent contradiction to force an audience to take stock of its moral stance and perhaps to adjust it, but with him it becomes almost an end in itself. By a curious reversal, the initial conflict in *Medea* is one where sympathy for the wronged heroine is greater today than it would have been in fifth century BC Athens, where Euripides was regarded, if Aristophanes is anything to go by, as something of a misogynist. Euripides, so modern in his sympathies, had to ensure that even an audience of Greeks would have been hard put to it to approve of this Jason.

In the first of his confrontations with the wife he is in the process of ditching in order to marry the King of Corinth's daughter, Jason coldly and rationally sums up the relationship with Medea as he sees it. In the first place Medea was quite unable to prevent herself helping Jason because of her love for him. He graciously allowed her to accompany him back from the wastes of Colchis to civilisation, where her gifts are more widely appreciated. His new marriage will be to the advantage of his and Medea's children, offering them security. Medea is wrong to get upset because of the interruption of their relationship. But, there, that's women.

The indignation that such sentiments naturally arouse today might suggest that *Medea* is an easy play. It is certainly a popular one, with more new productions in recent years, in a variety of production styles, than any other Greek tragedy or comedy, not to mention adaptations from Anouilh to Dario Fo. The original, though, does present some problems which will not simply evaporate by treating the play as a propagandist tract.

The opening is straightforward. The first character to appear is the Nurse, who reminds the audience of the circumstances which led to Jason and Medea arriving in Corinth. Jason has now betrayed Medea and she has reacted against him with a passion as powerful as that she formerly demonstrated in his interest. The Nurse is clear that Jason is in the wrong. She feels sympathy for Medea, though the power of her mistress's temper appals her.

The Tutor joins her, accompanied by the two children of Medea and Jason. Nurse and Tutor wag their heads at men's selfishness, as Medea is heard lamenting off-stage. The Chorus arrive, again sympathetic, again uncomfortable at Medea's extravagant reaction. By the time Medea does enter, her weeping has been replaced by an intensity that is far more chilling. It takes Creon, among the play's characters, to show any real awareness of Medea's true strength, and in the face of it he succumbs to her plea for time.

When Creon leaves the scene, the Chorus almost unwittingly find themselves accomplices in a course of action which is to lead to four murders, the last two infanticides of desperate savagery. This is not Medea's initial plan. Her first reaction is to kill Jason and his new wife, and she draws the Chorus in as fellow victims of men: 'The dawn of honour breaks for the race of women,' they sing, identifying their allegiance even before Jason has put in an appearance. When he does arrive, every word he says reinforces the dislike that an audience must feel for him. By the time he offers Medea letters of introduction to some of his friends, Euripides has almost made him a figure of fun, in the grisly black kind of way that will eventually see Pentheus as the butt of Dionysus in *The*

Bacchae. How can anyone be so blind as Jason, an audience might muse, at least half aware of how many of their acquaintances can be just as obtuse, if in less extreme circumstances. And, as when Pentheus berates Dionysus in *The Bacchae*, anticipation of the victim's revenge adds relish.

At this point the Chorus sing a surprisingly bland ode about the difficulties of falling in love and the misery of being a refugee. It is, though, more than an interlude to pass the time. There is a turning point here for the Chorus, still not aware (though the audience are beginning to realise) precisely where their natural sympathies are leading them.

The next scene tightens the knot. Out of the blue, Aegeus arrives from a visit to the oracle of Apollo. This sudden intervention from someone who can provide Medea with a bolt-hole has met with critical scorn over the years. Certainly there is no preparation for Aegeus' arrival and it is all too patently a matter of convenience for Medea and plot. But there is point to the scene which a whole view of the play brings out. Medea offers to help Aegeus over his childlessness in exchange for protection. Cautiously he agrees, on condition that she can make her own way to Athens.

Only when the play has run its course does it become apparent that this scene is more than a device for tying up ends. Aegeus' behaviour to Medea is on a par with that of everyone else; main characters, Chorus and probably audience. He is quite happy to appear to wave a liberal flag as long as it involves him in doing as little positive as possible, and if there is something in it for him. Aegeus, King of Athens as the audience are reminded, is a model of feckless diplomacy, our contemporary diplomacy no less than Athenian.

At the end of the play Medea appears to have extracted herself from her immediate situation by acquiring divine protection. She mentions in passing that she intends to settle in Athens, but by this time witch has become both seer and demi-goddess and is more than capable of looking after herself. The episode with Aegeus may seem isolated to someone attempting to apply to *Medea* the structure of a well-made play. Greek tragedy is seldom 'well-made'. Euripides is not alone among the Greeks in directi᷅ᵍ attention towards an issue from a series of perspectives. His *The Phoenician Women* offers a parallel, but others can be found in Aeschylus' *Prometheus* or Sophocles' *Oedipus at Colonus*. In each, the playwright builds a picture, the complete impression of which is of greater importance than an integrated plot. Because Euripides deals in reversals and recognitions in a manner that even Aristotle, no admirer of the *Medea,* would have acknowledged, detractors have been tempted to treat him as a simple story-teller, who worked himself into corners and who then extricated himself by damaging the story he was telling. Such a verdict is facile.

The practitioner, working on the production of a Euripides play, discovers soon enough that the purpose is not to manufacture a Chekhovian world in which any character is as interesting as any other. Myth dictated the outlines of the plot. What was fresh in Euripides was a determination to promote understanding. This is why his central figures can speak and react with real emotions, allowing the audience to be led gradually to see what motivates actions beyond their immediate comprehension. Medea murders her own children. How do you account for such an action? Euripides makes it possible not so much by enlisting sympathy for her crime as by forcing the audience to contemplate the circumstances in which it came to pass. Aegeus is as much a part of the 'civilised' world as is Jason, or indeed the Chorus, and his scene fits another piece in the jigsaw.

Only after he has departed does Medea reveal to the Chorus that her plan includes the murder of the two boys. Revenge against Jason, which was initially aimed at causing pain to him and his new wife, has veered off in another direction. It is a jolt for the audience who have so far been able to treat Medea with undiluted sympathy. 'Very well,' says the playwright, 'put your money where your mouth is and see if you are still so sure of your moral superiority.' The Chorus are caught in the same dilemma. So far they have gone along with Medea's plans. Now they are victims of the trap which catches most Greek choruses, though not often with such drastic consequences. They cannot get away until the play is over. No longer can they sit on the fence and sympathise with some hysterical threat. Either they inform on Medea, or they become accessories before the fact. In the hands of Euripides a convention becomes a moral pivot. Nor do they have long to think about it. After a brief ode in which they beg Medea to change her mind, and hence let them off the hook, Jason returns and Medea sets in train the sequence of murders.

Euripides brings back the children at this juncture and the reason can only be to drill home the point about what is now at stake. By the end of the scene Jason has been lulled into believing that his pragmatism has converted Medea, and the Chorus have lost their chance to intervene. The Tutor, who is not privy to Medea's plot, returns alone and reveals that the princess has accepted the poisoned robe. The die is cast. But is it? Medea is doomed, but the Tutor has the children with him and a single word from the Chorus could still save them. The Chorus keep quiet. Medea offers up her long and heart-rending speech of farewell to her sons. She takes them into the palace and the paralysed Chorus can do no more than sing a song about the joys and sorrows of having a family. It is no use suggesting, as some have, that the Chorus fail to act because choruses do not initiate action or break their given word. In a number of plays, from Aeschylus onwards, if circumstances demand it, they do affect the plot. Here Euripides draws attention to a lack of *will* to act, and in this resides the play's most telling message.

The horror of the death of Jason's new bride and her father, as related by the Messenger, is only a prelude to Medea's murder of the children off-stage, while the Chorus outside listen to their screaming. Jason returns, discovers what has happened and batters at the doors to Medea's house. What confronts him is not the expected tragic tableau wheeled on at ground level, but an epiphany, with Medea transfigured as she appears aloft in a winged chariot with the children's corpses and justifies her actions in a manner that looks forward to Dionysus' final appearance in *The Bacchae*.

The parallel to the later play does not stop here. Medea is a creature of passion, a passion which is beyond the comprehension of anyone else in the play. The 'rational' characters try to make allowance for her foreign ways and are wary of her witchery, except when it is convenient. Like Dionysus in *The Bacchae*, or Artemis and Aphrodite in *Hippolytus*, Medea is a fact of life.

Tangle with this sort of power and see what you get. Inevitably the play lends itself to being a platform for feminist opinion. Powerful enough at that level, it also makes a major contribution to Euripides' wider debate on human nature. He sets up a Greek Pinkerton and marries him to a hornet, not a butterfly. Loathe Jason as any audience must, the play has a deeper concern than watching a selfish pig get his come-uppance. Raw instinct, it tells us, and expedience are no match. Only by forcing the callous Jason to share her pain does Medea begin to make him realise what she is. The cool brutality of civilisation nurtures bloody destruction. There is the message, the implications of which every 'civilised' country in the world would be wise to heed.

The Phoenician Women

The story of Oedipus and his family is one that most of today's theatre-goers will feel they know. This puts them into a roughly similar position to the Athenian audience who first encountered *The Phoenician Women*. A modern audience will soon discover that they too are at the mercy of Euripides, who clearly did not believe that the last word had been said about that haunted king and his mother/wife.

By the time that Euripides presented *The Phoenician Women*, probably at the Great Dionysia of 409 BC, Aeschylus' *Seven Against Thebes* (467 BC) and two of Sophocles' Theban plays, *Antigone* (442 or 1 BC) and *Oedipus Tyrannus*, which is also known as *Oedipus Rex* or *Oedipus the King* (429 BC), had become 'classics', definitive versions to which all others would be referred. The Sophocles pair deal, in reverse chronological order, with events before and after those of *The Phoenician Women*. The Aeschylus play covers the same ground. Euripides might have seen the original *Seven Against Thebes* as a boy of about thirteen. He would almost certainly have been part of the first audience for *Antigone* and *Oedipus Tyrannus*. As the originality of Euripides gives his play its dramatic impetus, it is worth pointing initially to how he varied his inherited plot.

According to Sophocles, by the time Oedipus finally discovers that he has fulfilled the oracle which forecast that he would murder his father and marry his mother, Jocasta has already realised the truth and departed the scene to commit suicide. Oedipus finds her hanging and puts out his eyes. Creon assumes sole kingship and accedes to Oedipus' request that he be sent away from Thebes. There the *Oedipus Tyrannus* ends. Sophocles' *Oedipus at Colonus*, not yet written in 409 BC, covers Oedipus' arrival at Colonus, his last resting-place, and the remaining hours of his life. *Antigone,* the earliest performed, takes up the story again in Thebes, a city preserved from the horrors of civil way only by the death in single combat of Oedipus' sons, Eteocles and Polyneices, but torn apart once more by Creon's refusal to permit the burial of Polyneices and Antigone's defiant stand against him. Aeschylus' *Seven Against Thebes* features Eteocles and contains no other members of the family except Antigone and Ismene, who enter late to lament their brothers in a sequence which some modern critics consider spurious.

All this needs emphasing because *The Phoenician Women* has the feel – and by no means for the first time in Euripides – of being less an alternative view of the myth than a positive riposte to the work of the previous dramatists. He opens with a very much alive Jocasta – the first surprise – who gives her version of the past in a prologue speech to the audience. Here there are some minor variations from Sophocles relating to Oedipus' birth and upbringing, and a major one when it transpires that Oedipus killed Laius on the way *to* Delphi and then returned home to Corinth without ever receiving Apollo's oracle that he would kill his father and marry his mother. Whatever degree of blame may be attached to Oedipus by Sophocles, in Euripides he is absolved from any charge of having flouted Apollo's word.

When Oedipus discovered the truth about his marriage to his own mother, Jocasta continues, and his dual relationship with his four children, Eteocles, Polyneices, Antigone and Ismene, he blinded himself and was shut away by his sons. He is not now in exile, but living in the palace. Angry and humiliated, he has invoked a powerful curse on his sons and it is around this curse, that they should 'inherit from me the sword and the sword's edge', that the play revolves. Eteocles and Polyneices then made a deal that they should rule year and year about. When Eteocles' term as

King of Thebes was complete, he refused to hand over the throne. Polyneices has responded by raising an army to attack his native city. Here is another divergence from familiar Sophocles, though this time from the *Oedipus at Colonus*, still no more than a twinkle in the old man's eye. In Sophocles Polyneices is the elder brother, driven from Thebes by the younger Eteocles with whom no power-sharing deal has been struck. In *Seven Against Thebes* the brothers are regarded as twins, so that neither can lay claim to Thebes as his birthright. In Euripides, it is Eteocles who is the elder, though he declines to use this to justify his attitudes, and Polyneices who is their mother's undoubted favourite.

Aeschylus offers the point of view only of Eteocles in *Seven Against Thebes*, Sophocles that of Polyneices in *Oedipus at Colonus*, in a scene where he visits his father seeking a blessing for his attack on Thebes, a blessing which he singularly fails to get. Euripides tackles the issue with a head-on clash between the brothers, in a scene where the playwright seems to invite the audience to make a straight comparison with Aeschylus on the assumption that they will be familiar with the earlier play. One honour accorded to Aeschylus after his death, and apparently to no one else during the fifth century BC, was that his plays could be offered in revival as a festival entry. *Seven Against Thebes* was after all one of the plays that the 'dead' Aeschylus, as a character in Aristophanes' the *Frogs*, chose to quote in support of his case for being considered premier playwright in Hades. And the *Frogs* was performed only four years after *The Phoenician Women*.

This *ad hominem* approach of Euripides is in evidence on a number of occasions. The most celebrated is after Creon has suggested that the defence of the city be entrusted to a champion at each of the seven gates. In Aeschylus, single combat is proposed and each of the enemy champions is named and described so that Eteocles may find a suitable opponent, up to the final gate which Polyneices will attack with only Eteocles left to confront him. This selection of warriors occupies a full third of *Seven against Thebes*, as the tension mounts, Eteocles apparently unaware that his brother is one of the seven. Euripides has no time for such pussy-footing. 'I'll go round our seven gates, as you suggest,' he declares' 'and set a chosen man at each . . . I'll name them later – now would be wasting time.' Then for good measure he adds, 'But the one they set against me, god willing, will be my brother.' (748–51). The dig at Aeschylus is combined with a clear indication that the brothers have all along been spoiling for a fight.

The novelty of Euripides' approach is in the attention he draws to the dramatic method of his predecessors in order to deride it. Perhaps 'deride' is the wrong word. Parody would be more appropriate, and this is no isolated example. In *Electra*, Euripides' heroine is dismissive about the tokens by which brother and sister recognise one another in Aeschylus' parallel play, *The Libation-Bearers*. The echo is undeniable. In *Orestes*, Euripides points to the inconvenience of a singing and dancing chorus turning up when Electra has just succeeded in lulling her exhausted brother to sleep. Later in the same play a Messenger speech is delivered by a foreign slave in fractured Greek. Certainly this is closer to a parody of existing conventions than simply mockery of them. Perhaps even 'parody' underestimates the full purpose of Euripides. He is writing for a theatre tradition more than a hundred years old and for an audience whose increasing sophistication may be assumed from the sheer number of plays they may have witnessed, but who seemed to have grown morally and intellectually lazy. This is the method of an Ibsen or a Brecht, constantly challenging, often through the sly joke.

So much emphasis on the difference between this version of the story and others is more than academic juggling. Euripides inherited a theatre of stern, if not inflexible, conventions. He seems to have seen it as his duty, artistically, perhaps socially and politically too, to confront his audience with what they had come to take for granted and to surprise them from their complacency. Refinements to the plot, subtlety of motivation and frankness of expression all serve this end. *Seven Against Thebes* was the model for the patriotic statement on stage, combining a call for fortitude in the face of a common enemy with a warning against civic disruption. With the same story Euripides offered to a shattered and war-torn populace the complete destruction of a self-cursed family as an image of their own impending annihilation.

The Phoenician Women has always had its detractors, dismayed by, or at best apologetic about, its structure. Certainly there is a parade of incidents rather than an integrated plot: Antigone and the Tutor reviewing the army; Polyneices arguing his case with Eteocles; Teiresias forecasting disaster unless Creon's son is sacrificed; a first Messenger informing Jocasta and Antigone of Menoeceus' death; a second telling Creon of the deaths on the battlefield; Antigone's defiance of Creon; and finally Oedipus alone amidst the carnage. Professor Kitto, whose defence of the play was more spirited than most, suggested that it should be regarded as a 'pageant' or as 'very good cinema'. Defensive as this might sound, it does serve to give licence to a consideration of the play in its own terms rather than in those of Aristotle, or of any later critic who has seen fit to ascribe to Greek tragedy a rigid formula.

As it is written, and still more as it is performed, there is a perfectly good unifying factor that demolishes most of the complaints against the play's episodic nature. Jocasta, Antigone, Polyneices, Eteocles, Creon and Menoeceus are all part of one family:

> One blood, one race,
> Descended all
> From the horn'd moon-maiden, Io,
> We share one agony.

(l. 247–49)

This is a cursed house and the curse reaches into every last corner, to be shared, like it or not, by all who suffer the kinship. The initial curse was laid on Oedipus before he was born, an Oedipus blameless for the acts of parricide and incest, but responsible for reinforcing the gods' curse upon the heads of his sons with his own. Here is the biggest cast in any Greek tragedy and apart from a couple of messengers, a tutor and a prophet, they are all related to Oedipus. Not even the Chorus are exempt, tied, however tenuously, by blood to the house and caught up in the war by pure mischance. Oedipus is held back as a character until his nephew, his sons, and his mother/wife are all dead. Only then does the blind man enter to preside over the final scenes. Without even the consolation of exhausted quiet which marks the aftermath of many a tragedy, he has to listen to Creon threatening the life of his daughter who has pledged to bury Polyneices' body, while three other corpses lie at his feet. Antigone's reprieve, to escort her father into exile, is the prelude to the most pathetic of scenes, with Oedipus feeling for the faces of first Jocasta then his sons, for whose death he has been at least partly responsible.

Sophocles constructed a concentrated vision that has made of Oedipus a universal icon. To that extent *The Phoenician Women* will always suffer by comparison with *Oedipus Tyrannus*. With his opening prospect of a city under plague, Sophocles reflects the first years of the Peloponnesian War, for *Oedipus Tyrannus* was close in time to *Medea*. At least Sophocles shows something innately heroic in Oedipus' single-minded search for himself and in *Oedipus at Colonus* was to suggest the playwright himself coming to terms with the end of his life. Euripides' *The Phoenician Women* is from twenty years later, when any hope of an Athenian victory has been dissipated; when the curses of atrocity, deprivation and defeat have left no family in the land untouched; and when disaster can be laid at the door of human folly rather than divine displeasure. For Sophocles' Oedipus, exile and poverty await, but there will be a triumphant end, as he is summoned by the gods to transfiguration. If such an outcome is at the end of the road for Euripides' Oedipus, *The Phoenician Women* gives no hint of it. Here is only the despair of a playwright whose unhappy departure from his native land for ever was but a couple of years away.

In 409 BC, when the play was probably first presented, Athens was in the unusual position of having won two naval victories within two years, but Euripides cannot have been alone in realising that Athens was losing the war. The level of specific allegory contained in *The Phoenician Women* must evade a modern audience, but the warning it contains is modern enough. Disaster, however distant, leaves no one untouched. None of us can escape the curses inflicted on us by past generations, neither innocent idealist nor cynical in-fighter. Worse, the misery is compounded by the curses we inflict. Euripides' picture is a bleak one, created out of bleak times. He is today's playwright, writing plays for today.

The Bacchae

Greek tragedy is well endowed with people who inherit the fruits of their past actions. Jason initiated his own fate from the moment he first chose to use and abuse the love that Medea conceived for him. Oedipus was on a similar long fuse, one not primed by him, but ignited by the curse he called down on his sons. *The Bacchae* too concerns the legacy of the past and takes strands from both *Medea* and *The Phoenician Women*. Dionysus is an outsider, as is Medea, and he reacts to rejection with similar appalling results. He is at the same time a member of the ruling house of Thebes. His determination to reinstate himself leaves none of the rest of them untouched.

In each of the three plays in this volume the past catches up with the protagonists and the disintegration of family that results can all too easily appear as an image of the disintegration of society itself. *Medea* and *The Phoenician Women* both work as parable plays whose mythical ethos is no more than the bare bones of a story which is universal in its implications. *The Bacchae* resembles them in this, but possesses in addition a quality of mystery, which makes it quite unlike any other Greek drama. It is a mystery rooted in the identity of Dionysus himself.

Dionysus was god of the vine and of vegetation. He was also the god associated with the natural cycle and the changing seasons, the sufferer who died and was reborn. In this he preceded the Olympians and outlived them. Few cultures are without him in one form or another. His influence is perennial. To the Athenians there was the more specific aspect of his character, summed up in the title of E.R. Dodds' classic study, *The Greeks and the Irrational*. Dionysus was the god of ecstasy – ecstasy as a term to be taken literally, a 'standing outside of oneself' – and the god of unreason. This is the Dionysus of the faith-healer and the trance-dancer, of all those supra-normal powers which Teiresias notes and which so aggravate Pentheus by being beyond his explanation. The Dionysus of *The Bacchae* has at his disposal the power to derange. In his prologue speech to the audience he informs them that he has driven the women of Thebes mad, so that they now wander in the mountains, unaware of what they are doing. Later in the play his

power is seen at close quarters when he escapes from imprison-
ment and then bewilders Pentheus into dressing as a woman in
order to view for himself the Bacchic rites. When Pentheus'
mother Agave returns to the stage brandishing his head, she is still
under the influence of the god and has to be brought back to reality
by her appalled father.

The play offers several puzzles, paradoxes even, but one feature
is clear. Whether or not Pentheus, as King of Thebes, has any
right to try to restore normality to a situation that appears out of
control does not affect the nature of Dionysus' influence. Dionysus
exists. Apollo, a god of reason and harmony, may represent a saner
ideal, but the world is not notably sane and the Dionysiac can
break out at any time.

This factor alone is worth holding to when tackling what has
become a critical minefield. A bibliography on *The Bacchae* runs to
several hundred books and articles, many of them concerned with
promoting a case for either Dionysus or Pentheus as the party in
the right. 'Pentheus', one argument runs, 'is the fascist dictator,
wielding a blinkered authority and deserving anything that he
gets.' 'Dionysus', the King's apologists will counter, 'is a petty and
vindictive sadist whose vaunted freedom conceals a demoniac
coldness.' It is doubtful whether either extreme offers a tenable
interpretation of the piece as a whole. In pure dramatic terms there
is limited mileage, as even Aeschylus discovered, in the struggle
between saint and sinner. In the light of other Euripides plays,
something more subtle should be expected.

Euripides' world is not one in which moral decisions are easy,
and an audience's attitude to the protagonists may change as time
passes. Sure of themselves, the characters compete to be thought
sane, but sanity is not the prerogative of those who claim it. For
Euripides, moral certainty is linked to madness. When Dionysus
gets to work on the self-righteous Pentheus, he uncovers and
brings to the surface Dionysiac qualities within Pentheus, hitherto
dormant. Pentheus' moralising masks a deeper prurience, a
fascination with precisely those things he claims to deplore. 'One
thing more,' says Dionysus, as Pentheus threatens to call out the
troops against the women who have deserted Thebes to worship
their god, 'you would like to watch them up there in the

mountains, would you not?'

'Watch them?', replies Pentheus, 'Why, yes.' (*l.* 809–811) And he is hooked.

If Pentheus is shown to be morally fallible, a contributor to his own destruction, the ambiguity of Dionysus' motivation is likewise thrown into relief. What emerges in the scene where he reveals himself at last as a god – during the major part of the play he is 'disguised as a man' – is his human as opposed to his godlike nature. Everything relates back to his mother's rejection by her family.

Dionysus' mother was Semele, one of four daughters of Cadmus, the others being Agave, Ino and Autonoe. Seduced by Zeus, Semele became pregnant. Jealous Hera persuaded Semele to get Zeus to reveal himself to her in his proper form. She chose her moment to extract a promise on which Zeus could not renege and was burnt to a cinder for her pains. What Hera had neglected to tell her was that Zeus' real nature was a lightning-bolt. In the nick of time, though not for Semele, Zeus rescued the embryonic Dionysus and sewed him up in his thigh, from where in due course he was born. This unorthodox entry into the world is more bizarre than most births even in myth. Euripides is at some pains, perhaps with tongue in cheek, to offer, in the mouth of Teiresias, the contemporary Athenian sceptic's account of such a tale. But this was the story, and it is this divine aspect of Dionysus that Semele's sisters have denied. At the same time there is the human dimension. Whatever the full significance of the god's arrival in Thebes and his power to scramble the wits of his opponents, at the heart of the play there is, as in *Medea* and especially *The Phoenician Women*, a thoroughly domestic squabble, which provokes Dionysus' act of vengeance upon Cadmus and the rest of his kin.

The human part of Dionysus resents his exclusion from the family. Whatever the faults of Pentheus, and whether they should be attributed to youthful inexperience or a rather nasty nature, the warmth of feeling between him and his grandfather is undeniable. Pentheus castigates the prophet Teiresias as much for making his grandfather look a fool as for pursuing the Dionysiac cause. Cadmus has looked to Pentheus for protection ever since he abdicated in his favour. One of the most moving reversals in the play sees the old man restored to dignity as he returns with his beloved grandson's remains to face his gleeful daughter with the truth that the 'lion's head' she is brandishing is not what she thinks.

A break in the manuscript has robbed us of the exact words with which Dionysus returns to the scene, no longer *incognito*, but recognisable as the god. High above the action he reviews the ruins of the family to which he claims kinship. The amorality of the god part has disqualified him from the company of the family his human part seems to crave. The exchange between his grandfather and the god offers one of the play's most powerful moments:

CADMUS. We admit that we were wrong.
DIONYSUS. Too late. You acknowledge me far too late.
CADMUS. We know that, but you are too severe.
DIONYSUS. You offended me, me a god.
CADMUS. A god should not show passion like a man.

(*l.* 1343–1348)

The response sets even Dionysus back on his heels and gives emphasis to the sheer humanity of Euripides' approach to the story.

As in *The Phoenician Women*, it is the Chorus who give this play its title. In the earlier piece this takes some explaining, but in *The Bacchae* there is no difficulty. Tempting as some commentators have found it to treat this emphasis on the Chorus as a return to the Aeschylean pattern of *The Suppliants* or *Eumenides*, nothing else in Euripides suggests a playwright falling back on old devices. Quite the reverse. This chorus shows a stylistic advance on any other extant play, echoing the unseen chorus up in the hills and making the invisible visible. These Bacchants embody the Dionysiac religion itself in its total nature – peaceful, seductive, wilful, dangerous, malevolent, possessed. They are acolytes of the god, but simultaneously a corporate embodiment of his power. Their theatrical potential is as powerful as anything in the Greek theatre. Once this potential has been appreciated, many of the play's production problems evaporate. Even the earthquake which destroys Pentheus' place, a destruction to which the King makes no subsequent reference, is simply a demonstration of Dionysus' power seen through the eyes of his attendant Chorus.

As is clear from other plays, Euripides works with and around the mechanics of his theatre. In other tragedies, choruses of assorted slaves, suppliants and citizenry are variously excused, or tolerated, as part of an inherited dramatic structure. These Asian Bacchanals marry their true identity to their figurative being. Pentheus threatens them with prison as undesirable aliens for rampaging about in front of his palace, but the threat they pose as a living extension of Dionysus himself is one to which he is blind. Once only, at the entrance of Agave, do they suggest that they could feel pity and might perhaps, as human beings, dissociate themselves from Dionysus' vengeance. He is not present at the time and his timely reappearance restores their allegiance. An audience, initially sympathetic to the Dionysus oppressed by his regimented cousin and in harmony with the gentler sentiments of the Chorus, will find themselves by the end no longer able to subscribe to the mayhem the god has initiated. Echoes from the *Medea* are irresistible.

Perhaps all this seems too much like prescribing a 'correct' view, undesirable with a play of such breadth and complexity. There can never be a definitive *The Bacchae*. There are, though, undeniable turning-points in the text, as there are in *Medea* and *The Phoenician Women*, where the audience are forced to reappraise. Euripides is crafty at engineering turns of event which make things appear in a new light. Pentheus versus Dionysus may be a simple collision between temporal and spiritual priorities. That collision can provide a starting point for a thematic dissection of *The Bacchae*, but it is no more than a starting point for a play whose richness is a constant source of wonder.

The Bacchae, like most great plays, is a number of things at once and intertwines ideas at differing levels of perception, each or any of which may dominate in different productions or for different members of a single audience. It is a play in which illusion wrestles with reality, a play about the quality of religious experience, about maleness and femaleness and the nature of sexuality, a black comedy, a family saga, a revenge tragedy, a threat to society, a plea for compassion. In other words it is one of that small and select

band of plays against which all the rest, and not only from the Greek repertoire, must be judged. A formidable intellectual challenge, its substance is the demolition of intellect, argument and reason in the face of a power beyond analysis. That power is at least in part the power of the theatre itself where Dionysus is truly a god, able to make the scalp creep and the throat tighten.
The Bacchae is Euripides' tribute to theatre.

The line-numbering alongside the texts relates to the Greek original rather than the English translations.

J. Michael Walton, 1987

MEDEA

Translated by Jeremy Brooks

Characters

NURSE to Medea
TWO SONS of Jason and Medea
TUTOR to the children
THREE WOMEN of Corinth
MEDEA
CREON, King of Corinth
JASON
AEGEUS, King of Athens
MESSENGER
SERVING WOMEN
SOLDIERS

This translation was first performed by the Theatr Clwyd
Company in The Theatr Clwyd, Mold, on 31 January 1986,
with the following cast:

NURSE	Anne Dyson
TWO SONS	James Hussaney, Stephen Evan
TUTOR	Christopher Burgess
THREE WOMEN	Beejaye, Sharon D. Clarke, Claudette Williams
MEDEA	Eileen Atkins
CREON, King of Corinth	Clifton Jones
JASON	Leon Herbert
AEGEUS, King of Athens	Paul Barber
MESSENGER	Leo Wringer
SERVING WOMEN and SOLDIERS	Stuart Mannix, Darren Swallow

Designer	Simon Higlett
Composer	Anthony Ingle
Movement Co-ordinator	Terry John Bates
Director	Toby Robertson

Notes

This version of MEDEA was prepared for a specific production.
The intended style of the production was discussed at length by
writer and director before work on the text began, so this is
very much an 'acting version' which has been refined in the
rehearsal room. Sometimes such 'refinements' lead to
inaccuracy; where this had happened I have restored my original
solutions for the published text. The production later
transferred to the Young Vic in London.

Passages surrounded by square brackets indicate cuts that
were made during rehearsals, usually for reasons of dramatic
rhythm.

Before the Palace of CREON *at Corinth.*

NURSE. O all you gods, why did you let
    The good ship Argo find a safe way through
    The mist-blue rocks that guard the gate to Colchis?
    Why did you let the pines of Pelion
    Fall to the woodman's axe to furnish oars
    For those who went to fetch the golden fleece?
    O all you gods, where were you then?
    I wish these things had never happened!

    For then Medea, my dear mistress,
    Mad with love for Jason,
    Would never have sailed with him to Hellas;
    Would never have tricked the daughters of King Pelias
    Into their father's murder; would never have fled
    To this strange city with Jason and his sons.
    She came to Corinth an exile and a stranger
    And found a welcome here. To Jason she has given   10
    The obedience that secures a peaceful home.
    But now that love has turned to hatred.
    The tender ties are broken and wrenched apart.
    Jason has betrayed my mistress
    By taking to his bed a royal young bride,
    Daughter to Creon, king of this land.
    And now my princess, scorned, invokes the oaths
    That Jason swore for her, recalls the pledge
    Given by his strong right hand   20
    And bids all heaven to witness
    How Jason has valued her service and her love.

    And now she lies in there
    Abandoned to her grief.
    She will not eat,
    She will not sleep.

She lets her tears
Wash time away. So she has been
Since she first heard of this betrayal.
She lies there shattered, still; a stricken rock
Or frozen ocean wave; she will not lift
Her eyes to see the world, she will not raise
Her head up off the ground, she will not hear
The warnings of her friends; but only sways
30   Her snow-white neck slowly from side to side
Moaning the loss of father, country, home,
Which she gave up to follow faithfully
The man who now dishonours her and them.
She learns too late, my poor princess,
How foolish it is
To turns one's back upon one's native land.

She hates her children now. She has no joy
In seeing them, and I am full of fear.
Violence moves in her heart.
I know this woman well, and dread
40   The thoughts that stir in her. Her wrath
Is awesome. The man that earns her hate
Will never hurt her pride and go unscathed.

Look where her children come
Hot from their playing still,
Their mother's grief forgotten.
The soul of a child is a stranger
To sorrow and danger.
Enter TUTOR and the two CHILDREN.
TUTOR. Why, Nurse, what are you doing, crouching
50   Here in the courtyard alone, repeating
Your melancholy tale? Surely our mistress
Should not be left on her own?
NURSE. Old man, I have served our princess as a nurse
Since she was a child, as you have as a tutor.
Loyal slaves must grieve and wring their hearts
When grave misfortune strikes their masters.

6

I could not resist my longing to come out
And tell all heaven and earth
Our mistress's hard fate.

TUTOR. What! Has our mistress not stopped moping yet?

NURSE. Stopped moping? What do you think? 60
She is only at the beginning of her grief.

TUTOR. Poor fool – I shouldn't speak so but I must –
She little knows how great her grief will be.

NURSE. She little knows – ? What do you mean? Tell me.

TUTOR. Nothing. I wish I hadn't spoken.

NURSE. No, old man. We are both slaves.
You can safely confide in me.

TUTOR. I was passing the place where the old men sit
Playing at draughts, near the Pirean spring.
Pretending not to listen, I overheard one say
That Creon, who rules this land, is now intent 70
On driving Medea and her children
Out of his country. But I don't know
Whether the rumour is true. I hope it's false.

NURSE. Surely lord Jason could never accept
His children's banishment, however much
He may be at odds with their poor mother?

TUTOR. Old ties give way to new. The lord Jason
No longer loves his family.

NURSE. Then there's no hope for us, if we must add
New woes to ones we've so far barely tasted.

TUTOR. But you must keep quiet about these things. 80
This is no time for our mistress to hear of them.

NURSE. Oh children, do you hear
How your father has changed towards you?
May he be damned! – No, no, he is still my master!
And yet – yet – he is still a traitor!

TUTOR. What man is not? Are you only now
Learning that all men love themselves
More than their neighbours?
Some out of greed; but even the honest
Love themselves for their own honesty.
Jason spurns his old family

To gain a new advantage.

NURSE. Go into the house, children. All will be well.

90   Keep them from their mother's sight, old man.
Don't bring them near her in her evil mood.
She eyes them balefully, as if to do them harm.
I know her fury will not rest
Until she has pounced on her chosen victim.
Heaven let her choose an enemy, not a friend.

MEDEA (*off*). Oh! Oh! What wretchedness! What misery!
Oh how I wish I was dead!

NURSE. There, you can hear for yourselves.
Your mother's heart is racked with fancies,

100   Goaded by furies. Into the house, children,
Into the house quickly, and stay away
From your mother, don't let her see you,
Do not approach her while this mad mood lasts,
While her reckless heart rides out this tempest.
In, in with you, quickly.
Exit TUTOR and CHILDREN.
These cries are only the heralds of a storm
Whose lightning soon will strike.
What sin will this proud restless soul commit

110   Out of the depths of her anguish?

MEDEA (*off*). Oh! Oh! Oh I have suffered
More agony than all these tears can show.
Curse you, you damned children,
Curse your father and curse your doomed mother!
Let ruin seize the whole house!

NURSE. Oh no, no! For pity's sake, why must
The children suffer for their father's sin?
Why hate them? Poor babes, I fear for you!
The tempers of the great are strange and dangerous.

120   Because they have never learned to obey,
Only to command, it is difficult
To move them from their moods.
It is better to have learned to live as equals.
I want no greatness crowning my old age,
Only peace and security.

Moderation in all things is best for man.
Greatness brings more misery than joy
And pays a higher price when the gods frown. 130
CHORUS. I heard the voice,
I heard the cry
Of the foreign princess.
I stood by the double gates
Heard wild weeping within
And I grieve for this house's pain
For it has won my love.
NURSE. It is a house no longer.
As a house it has passed away.
A new bride keeps Jason at her side 140
And my lady mourns her loss alone,
Deaf to the comfort of friends.
MEDEA (*off*). Oh let the lightning strike
And break my head in two!
What do I want with a life
That is all woe, and woe, and woe?
Let me be free of it!
CHORUS. Oh Zeus, did you hear,
Oh Earth, oh Light, did you hear
The cries of this stricken woman?

Poor restless heart, why yearn 150
For the insatiable grave?
Death will come when it comes.
No need to pray for it.

Your partner now lusts for young love.
Spend no more feeling on him.
Zeus will judge between you.
Do not waste your womanhood
Grieving for the loss of a man.
MEDEA (*off*). Great Zeus, father of gods and men,
And Themis, guardian of righteousness, 160
See what I suffer now, even though I bound
My accursed husband to me in your names!

Oh, let me see him and his bride destroyed
And all his house brought down in ruins
For rewarding my loyalty with this black shame!
Oh my father, my country, it was for this I left you
With my brother's blood upon my hands!

NURSE. Do you hear how wildly she invokes
170   The guardians of men's oaths?
No small revenge can come of such a rage.

CHORUS. If only she would come out here
To see us, if only she would listen
To our advice, if only she would put aside,
For a moment, the curtain of her passion!

I cannot deny help
To those I regard as friends.
180   Go into the house, Nurse,
And ask her to come out to us.

Yes, hurry, Nurse, before she does
Some harm to those inside.
This grief of hers is mounting
Like an angry wave.

NURSE. I am content to try, but do not think
My mistress will listen to me. She looks at us,
Whenever we draw near, like a lioness
Guarding her new-born cubs . . .

190   The minstrels of old were foolish.
I think they wasted their time
Composing their songs to grace
A feast, or inventing a rhyme
To please the ear at a dance
And make life seem sublime.

For none of them ever tried
To use their music to ease
The griefs to which man is prone,
The misfortunes that never cease

When families are overthrown
And discord destroys our peace.

Surely it would be a gain
If music could ease man's pain?   200
The NURSE goes in.

CHORUS. I heard that bitter cry
Of grievous wrong, I heard her call
Curses on the traitor of her marriage bed.

I heard her invoke bright Themis,
Bride of Zeus, who witnessed
The oaths that brought her here
To fair Hellas from the far Asian shore,   210

Witnessed the promises that led her from her home,
Across that dark unfriendly sea
And through the bottomless salt straits that guard
The entrance to our boundless ocean here.
Enter MEDEA.

MEDEA. Women of Corinth. I have come
To speak with you. I would not have you
Condemn me as unfriendly. Many great people,
Both those who live in seclusion and those
Who lead a public life, I know are blamed
For being proud, or indifferent to others' feelings.
Often this is unjust. One may be condemned
On sight, before one's real nature is known.   220
A stranger, most of all, should try to learn
And then adopt the manners of his hosts.
Even a citizen should not resist,
From stubbornness or pride, his city's ways.

I stand before you then, a stranger who
Is struck down by disaster. Quite suddenly
My life's destroyed. I only wish to die.
Kind friends, you know
That he who was my world,

11

Whom I called husband,
Has now betrayed me.

230   Of all earth's creatures
We women are the most unfortunate.
First we must secure a husband
At an exorbitant price
And then to make a bad deal worse
We set him up as tyrant over our bodies
And only then discover
Whether we've made a good choice or a bad one.
Divorce is not respectable for a woman;
Nor can she, having wed, repel the man.
Next must the wife learn new ways and new customs,
Lessons not taught at home,
And she will need
The eye of a diviner, magical arts,
240   To see how best to treat this strange new partner.
If with good luck we manage to perform
Our tasks with thoroughness and tact
So that our man stays with us without struggling
Against the marriage yoke, then all is well.
If not, it were best to die.
For when a man grows tired of life at home
He'll leave and seek some friend of his own sex
To help him rid himself of his disgust,
While we can only feed on the one man.

And yet men say, with sorry reasoning,
That women live secure and safe at home
While they are at the wars. Yet I would rather
250   Stand three times in the front line of a battle
Than once give birth to a child.

But enough of that. Thoughts like these
Do not apply to you as they do to me.
You have your city. You have your father's house,
You have your friends to share the joys of life,

While I have nothing. I have no city,
And so my husband can scorn me
As no more than passing booty
Won in a foreign land. I have no mother,
No brother, no kinsman to protect me
In my extremity. So I have one request:
If I can find some way to avenge myself   260
On my husband for his cruelty
Or on the king, or on the bride herself,
Then I ask only this, women of Corinth:
Your silence. We women are timorous creatures,
We shrink from the sight of steel.
Yet when a woman's honour is defiled
No heart is flooded with a deadlier will.
CHORUS. I can promise you silence, Medea.
　　You have a right to your revenge.
　　Your angry grief is no surprise.
　　But look, I see Creon, our King, approaching
　　Herald of some new decree.   270
　　Enter CREON
CREON. Medea, you with your lowering looks,
　　You, Medea, with your venomous thoughts,
　　I banish you, Medea. You will take
　　Yourself and your two children from my land,
　　Take yourself into exile. No delays.
　　I am the judge in this. That is my sentence.
　　I shall not return to my palace until I've seen
　　You banished from the borders of my land.

MEDEA. Oh, now it comes! The bitter end is here.
　　My enemies bear down upon me in full sail
　　And no safe harbour offers hiding-place.
　　Yet in all my misery I ask you,   280
　　Creon, why do you drive me from your land?
CREON. I fear you, Medea. I no longer need
　　To hide my fear. I fear you may
　　Have plans to harm my daughter.
　　I have many reasons for my fear.

13

You have been a sorceress from birth,
Expert in many evil arts,
And you are seething at the loss of Jason.
I hear too that you have threatened me,
The father of the bride, as well as Jason
And the bride herself.
Therefore I must take action now, before
You can make mischief for us. It is better
290   For me to earn your hatred now, Medea,
Than weaken my resolve, and live to rue it.
   MEDEA. Alas! Creon, this is not the first time
My reputation has served me badly.
Wise men should never bring their children up
To be too clever. It only earns
The envy of those who struggle to compete.
If you try to teach
Some new ideas to fools, they'll only damn
Your shallow ignorance; while if you get a name
300   For being wiser than the established sages
You'll earn their hatred too. This has been my lot.
Some think me clever and dislike me for it,
To others I am proud without good cause.
And you – you are afraid that I'll upset
The decent harmony of your arrangements.

You need not fear me, Creon. Why should you?
How can I hurt a king? Why should I?
How have you injured me? You have betrothed
Your daughter to the man who suits you
As you have every right to do. It's true.
310   I hate my husband for it, but not you.
You have done wisely and deserve your happiness.
Marry your child to Jason, and good luck to you.
But let me still live in Corinth. I have been wronged,
But I will bear with it, and keep my place.
   CREON. Your words are meek, Medea; yet I dread
The mischief in your heart. I trust you now
Less than before. It is easier to take guard

14

Against hot temper than against sweet reason. 320
No, you must go at once. I'll listen
To no more speeches. The order is given.
No cunning now can keep you in this city.
I know you hate me.
MEDEA. No, Creon, I beg you! Look, I am on my knees!
By the soul of your sweet daughter, I beseech you!
CREON. Your words are wasted. You'll never change my mind.
MEDEA. Will you banish me, then, without a moment's pity?
CREON. I will. It is my family I love, not you.
MEDEA. Oh my country, my country, how I yearn for you now!
CREON. Yes. I too love my country. But my child,
My child I love above all things.
MEDEA. Ah, what a scourge to mortal men is love. 330
CREON. I think our differing fortunes govern that.
MEDEA. Oh Zeus, remember who caused all my despair!
CREON. Go, go, you passionate fool,
And free me from these cares.
MEDEA. The cares are all mine. I have enough of them.
CREON. Then take them far from here. My men will see to it.
MEDEA. Not that, not force: I do entreat you, Creon!
CREON. I see you're still bent on making a disturbance.
MEDEA. No, no, I'll go. It was not that I begged for.
CREON. Then why this show of passion? Why don't you leave?
MEDEA. Allow me to remain for this one day 340
To make plans for my exile, to make provision
For my children. Their father will not do it.
Oh, pity my sons! You too have children, Creon,
Which surely must dispose you towards kindness.
I care nothing for myself, nor for my exile,
But for my sons I weep, for they will learn
The meaning of sorrow.
CREON. I am not a harsh man. I have often shown pity
And sometimes had to pay the price for it.
And now, although I see the folly of it,
I'll grant you this request, Medea. But be warned:
If the first rays of tomorrow's sun
Find you and your children still within my borders

You will die. I give my word on that.
So, if you must, stay this one day only:
Not time enough to do the things I dread.
Exit CREON.
CHORUS. Alas! Medea, what sorrows beset you!
Where, where can you turn;

What home, what country, can you find
360   To protect you from these troubles?

Oh Medea, on what a hopeless sea
Of misery the gods have launched you!
MEDEA. Yes, yes, I am hemmed in on every side.
But don't imagine all my battles lost.
I can deal trouble too.
Trouble is looming for this young bride,
And for the bridegroom, a whole sea of it.

Do you think I would have fawned on that man there
Without some purpose? No, I would never
370   Have spoken to him, let alone touched him!
But if he had banished me today, as he intended,
My plans would have been ruined. Well, luckily
He's fool enough to grant me this one day –
Enough to devise a fate for these three enemies,
Father and daughter, and my faithless husband.

I have thought of so many ways to kill them,
My friends, I am at loss to choose.
Shall I set fire to the bridal chambers?
Or steal into the bedroom where the sheets enfold them
380   And plunge the sharp sword through their pumping hearts?
The danger there is that I might be caught
And killed myself before my sword has spoken,
Leaving the last laugh to my enemies.
No, I will not be mocked; give them no chance
To make the name Medea a laughing stock.
The simplest way is best, the way

16

We women are most skilled at,
The way of poison.

Well, now: suppose them dead.
What city will receive me? What host
Offer me friendly shelter, a home
And sanctuary? There's none.
I've gained a little time, so I will stay
My hand a little while, and hope to find
Some new ally to offer me a refuge.   390
Then I could do my murders with quiet cunning.
But if I'm banished with no hope of safety
I'll seize the sword in my own hand
Even if I die for it, and kill them,
Yes, go out boldly to the kill, and kill.

By Hecate, the fearsome Queen of the Underworld,
Whom I revere above all other gods,
Whom I have chosen as my task's accomplice,
By Hecate, the secret guest of my soul,
Not one of these shall soil my honour
And fail to pay for it.
They shall repent their marriage
In bitterness and pain; bitterly repent
Their wooing, bitterly repent my banishment.   400

Come then, Medea!
Plot and scheme,
Use all your magical arts,
Now comes the testing time,
Up, and on to the danger!
Remember what you have suffered and still suffer.
You cannot let this royal Corinthian house,
The race of Sisyphus, use Jason's wedding
To mock Medea, daughter of a king
Sprung of Helios the Sun-god.
You have cunning enough. Besides,
We that are born women

17

Though little apt for noble deeds
To fashion mischief are most expert.
CHORUS. Back to their sources
Run the holy rivers,
Order and the world
410   Stand upside down.
Now it is men whose words are treacherous,
Now it is men whose oaths the gods disown.

The dawn of honour breaks
For the race of women.
Slander's poisoned tongue
Shall stab at us no more.
420   The faithlessness of women – that old theme –
No longer ease the minstrel's daily chore.

Phoebus, the lord of minstrels,
Withheld from women
The gift of heavenly song.
Had I such powers
I'd answer men's complaint, for time contains
As many themes on their sex as on ours.

You left your father's house
With your heart enflamed,
430   Sailed through the sea's twin rocks
To a foreign strand.
Now your bed's empty and your name dishonoured,
Yourself reviled and exiled from this land.

Gone is the grace
That oaths once had.
Through all of Hellas
Honour is found no more.
Honour is fled to Heaven, and you are left,
440   Homeless and fatherless upon an alien shore.

While over your home presides another queen,

The new young bride now being what you had been.
Enter JASON.

JASON. This is by no means the first time I have noted
The destructive effect of an unruly temper.

You, Medea, might have stayed here in this land,
Even in this house, if you had bowed
Submissively to the wishes of your rulers,
But now your thoughtless words have banished you.   450

You can revile Jason as the worst of men
As much as you want; but having spoken ill
Of the King and his daughter,
You must count your life a bonus,
Mere exile your good fortune.
At all times I have tried to modify
The fury of the King, and would have kept you here.
But you would not forego your childish rages
Went on reviling them: and so are banished.

Yet even after all this, I'll not desert you.
My good will continues. I am come to you now
Having taken much thought for your future.   460
So that you and your sons will not be destitute
Or want for anything when you are exiled,
For exile brings a host of troubles with it.
However badly you may think of me, Medea,
I shall never bear ill will towards you.

MEDEA. You come to me, you coward! – that's the only name
My tongue can find that's foul enough
For you and your unmanliness!
You come to me! You, whom the gods despise,
Hated by me, hated by all mankind,
You come to me! Oh, it's no proof
Of courage or audacity to confront
Friends you have injured; it's that worst   470
Of man's diseases, total loss of shame.
Yet you've done well to come. Reviling you

Will ease my soul a little; and listening
Will make you suffer.

I shall begin at the very beginning.
As every hero of Hellas knows
Who sailed with you aboard the Argo,
When my father sent you
To tame the fire-breathing bulls, and yoke them,
And sow the deadly field with dragon's teeth
I saved your life!
Yes! And it was I who slew the serpent
480   Who wreathed his coils about the Golden Fleece,
Guarding it sleeplessly, yes, it was I who raised
The torch of your success!

My father and my home I left
To come with you to Iolchos
Below Mount Pelion, because my love for you
Was stronger than my prudence. Next, I tricked
The daughters of King Pelias, your rival,
Into encompassing his dreadful death.
All this I did for you.
For you, you traitor!
You, who have cast me off,
Taking a new wife even though
I have given you two sons!
490   Had you been childless still
I might have sympathised with your desire
For a new marriage.

My trust in oaths is shattered.
I do not even understand
Whether you think the gods that you once swore by
Still rule mankind, or if perhaps some new authority
Is now in fashion? Doesn't your own conscience tell you
That you have not kept faith with me?

Ah! poor right hand

Which you so often pressed . . .!
These knees . . .! I've been polluted
By the touch of a traitor.
All my bright hopes
Fallen to dust.

But let me ask your advice
As if you were a friend.
I can expect no help
From someone as villainous as you,   500
And yet I'll do it.
My questions will expose
The true depths of your villainy.

Tell me, where can I turn now?
To my father's house, my country
Which I betrayed to follow you?
To the unhappy daughters of King Pelias
Whose death I engineered?
A fine welcome I'd have there.
My case, then, is just this:
I have become the bitter foe
Of my own homeland
For your sake. I have gained the enmity
Of harmless friends
For your sake. For my reward I'm seen
By women everywhere as truly blessed –   510
Possessor of an unparalleled loyal lord –
So loyal, for pity's sake, he'd cast me out,
Friendless, an exile,
A woman, with two children, all alone!

Yes, it's a nice reproach
To you on your marriage day
That your two fine sons
And the woman who saved your life
Should be beggars and vagabonds!

O Zeus! Why give us the skill
To tell true gold and fake apart
While no man's brow is clearly marked
To show he has a serpent's heart?

520 CHORUS. Quarrels are terrible
And never to be mended
Between lovers once united
Whose love has ended.

JASON. It seems that I must now turn orator
And like a helmsman on a close-reefed ship
Weather the storms your tiresome tongue blows up.
Since you exaggerate your service to me
I have to tell you that my safe return
From all my travels was, as I believe,
The work of Aphrodite, and of her alone.
You are a clever woman, Medea; perhaps it would be
530 Unkind to insist that it was only the Love-god's
Irresistible shaft that forced you
Into saving my life. And so I will not
Labour the point. However you came to serve me
It was as well you did.

But in return for saving me I can show
That you received more than you gave.
First, instead of living among barbarians
In your barbarian land, you live in Hellas.
You have learned what Justice means
And how the rule of Law's superior
To that of brute force. The people of Hellas
Recognise your gifts; you have won
540 A name for yourself, a reputation.
If you had stayed there, on the edge of the world,
No tongue would ever have learned to say Medea!
No hoard of gold, no skill to sing
A better song than Orpheus ever sang
Is worth considering until one's fame's secure!
I'll say no more about our history
And only this because you challenged me.

As for your reproaches about my marriage,
I can show, first, that it was prudent,
Second, that it was not prompted by passion,
Third, that it should have been to your advantage
And to the advantage of our sons.

No, quiet a moment! Since I was forced   550
To seek asylum in this land of Corinth,
What better outcome could an exile hope for
Than marriage to the daughter of the King?
It was not because I had grown tired of you –
That thought seems most to rankle –
Nor because I lusted for a young bride,
Nor because I longed to have more children:
The sons we have are enough, I have no complaint.
No, it was my first, my most important aim
That we should live in comfort, not in poverty
(I know too well how friends avoid the poor)   560
And my sons be brought up as their rank deserves.
I also hoped to have new heirs, as brothers
To those that you have borne, and raise our sons
To the same high rank, uniting
Two families into one, that all might prosper.
You need no more children, certainly,
But it would have benefited those we have
For me to have more by this new alliance.
Am I not right in this? Even you
Would say so if you were not stung
By sexual jealousy. No, but you women
Have such strange ideas; you seem to think
That if your sexual rights are not infringed
Then everything is well. But if some little thing   570
Ruffles your ownership, then all that once was good,
All that was valuable, means nothing to you.
It would be better for the human race
If children could be born
Without the need for women.
Mankind would have been spared a host of evils.

CHORUS. Jason, your speech is cleverly contrived,
    Yet still I think, however indiscreet
    My words may seem, it is a sin to treat
    Your wife like this, and cruelly cast her out.
MEDEA. No doubt I differ from others in many ways.
580   To me, the man with skill to fence with words
    In an unjust cause should be the more condemned.
    So sure that he can cast a decent veil
    Of pompous righteousness over his foul deeds,
    He pursues them all the more vigorously.
    And yet he's not so clever after all.

    No, I can shatter your glib defence
    With a single thought. If you had anything
    But a serpent's heart, you would have come to me
    With your proposals, sought my consent
    Before you made your match, instead of hiding it
    From those who loved you.
JASON. And you, no doubt, would then have lent me
    All your support for my proposed marriage –
590   You, who cannot hide your soul's hot fury!
MEDEA. That was not what restrained you.
    You have been looking towards old age
    When it would not be respectable to have
    A barbarian for a wife.
JASON. Be sure of one thing: it was not because
    Of the woman herself that I made
    This royal marriage, but, as I've told you,
    To ensure your future, and to be
    The father of royal sons bound by blood
    To those I had by you, for our security.
MEDEA. I want no security that ends in woe
    Nor wealth that's bought with agony of heart.
600 JASON. You would be wise to see this differently.
    You should not consider painful
    What is good for you; nor, when fortune smiles,
    Pretend she frowns.
MEDEA. Now you mock me: you have a refuge here,

I am alone, an exile from tomorrow.

JASON. By your own choice. You've no one else to blame.

MEDEA. What did I do? Swear loyalty to you, then betray you?

JASON. You invoked the gods' curses on the King's house.

MEDEA. Perhaps on your house too I shall bring a curse.

JASON. Enough of this. I will dispute
These points no further. Now tell me
If you will take some part of my new fortune   610
To support the children and yourself in exile?
I will give it gladly. Yes, and I will send
Messages to friends abroad
That they should treat you well.
You would be foolish to refuse this offer.
Master your anger for your greater gain.

MEDEA. I'll have no dealings with your friends.
I'll take nothing from you, so offer nothing.
The gifts of a traitor
Are tainted with treachery.

JASON. Then let the gods here witness my readiness
To help you and our sons; let them see   620
How you refuse me, and turn from your friends
In stubbornness, making your hard lot worse.

MEDEA. Leave me, Jason. Go. You are inflamed
With love for your young bride. You have lingered
Too long away from her chamber.
Go to her. If the gods allow,
You shall have such a wedding day
As any man might shrink from.
  Exit JASON.

CHORUS. When love descends on man in brash excess
Hot past all limits
Nothing of glory nor good will come of it
Though if love's queen in gentleness approach,   630
Moderate, restrained,
No goddess is so full of starry charm.
O Aphrodite, goddess, never bend
Your golden bow toward me, nor loose
Your passion-poisoned dart

At this weak heart.

Let chastity, the fairest gift of heaven,
Protect and favour me.
May the dread goddess never clamp on me
The hot iron jaws of restless jealousy
Nor smite my temper
With mad desires to follow fresher loves.
O Aphrodite, goddess, always bless
The peace of marriage, and choose well for us
640   So we may keep the bed
Of those we wed.

O my dear country, sweetest native city,
May the gods grant
I never shall be outcast from my home
To lead that pointless, empty, wandering life,
Each day a misery
Of cruellest torment. O you great gods,
Before that happens let me yield to death,
650   Yes, let death take me first!
Bitterer than bile
Are the dregs of exile.

This is no lesson learned from the lips of others.
It is before my eyes.
You have no city, Medea, you have no friend
To pity you in your great emptiness,
To hold you dear,
No one to turn to in your lonely grief.
Oh you great gods, let him die in dishonour
660   Who keeps no faith with loved ones
Nor seeks to make amends.
He has no friends.
Enter AEGEUS.

AEGEUS. All happiness, Medea! There is no better greeting
Between old friends than this.

MEDEA. All happiness to you, Aegeus,

26

[Son of Pandion, the wise] King of Athens.
Where have you been, that brings you here?

AEGEUS. I come from the old oracle of Apollo.

MEDEA. What did you seek at earth's prophetic centre?

AEGEUS. To ask how I might be blessed
With children of my own seed.

MEDEA. Are you then still without children? 670

AEGEUS. A visit from Poseidon so ordained it
That Theseus, my heir, is not my son.

MEDEA. [You have a wife. Do you not bed with her?

AEGEUS. My wife and I enjoy the rights of marriage.]

MEDEA. And what advice had the oracle for you?

AEGEUS. Words too subtle for a mortal to understand.

MEDEA. Is it proper for me to hear the god's answer?

AEGEUS. Certainly. Yours is just the intelligence it needs.

MEDEA. What did the god say? Am I to hear?

AEGEUS. I was instructed 'not to unstop
The wineskin's pendant neck'.

MEDEA. The god means you to stay chaste. Did he say 680
For how long, or what country you must visit first?

AEGEUS. Until I have returned to my native land.

MEDEA. [Then for what purpose have you sailed to Corinth?

AEGEUS. You know of Pittheus, the King of Troezen?

MEDEA. King Pelop's son? A learned man they say.

AEGEUS. And father to my wife. I shall seek from him
Advice about the oracle's command.

MEDEA. The man is shrewd and expert in such lore.

AEGEUS. Yes, and my dearest friend in battles past.]

MEDEA. Then all good luck to you, and all success.

AEGEUS. But why so downcast, Medea?
Why these pale and wasted cheeks?

MEDEA. Oh, Aegeus, my husband has turned out a traitor! 690

AEGEUS. [What do you mean! Tell me what has happened.

MEDEA. Jason has betrayed me, and without cause.]

AEGEUS. What has he done? Tell me more plainly.

MEDEA. He has taken another wife, displacing me
As mistress of his house.

AEGEUS. Could Jason, of all men, do such a thing?

27

MEDEA. It is certain that he has. Once he loved me
    But now I am disowned.
AEGEUS. Did he fall in love? Or out of love with you?
MEDEA. Oh yes, the traitor, he has fallen in love.
AEGEUS. If he is such a villian, then be done with him.
700   MEDEA. He is in love with marriage to a royal house.
AEGEUS. Why, who has offered him his daughter?
MEDEA. It is Creon, King of this land of Corinth.
AEGEUS. Then, Medea, your grief is justified.
MEDEA. Yes, I am ruined. And more – I am banished too.
AEGEUS. Every word brings worse news! Who has banished you?
MEDEA. Creon is bent on driving me from Corinth.
AEGEUS. And Jason accepts this? That would be truly shameful.
MEDEA. He made a show of protest, but will not resist it.
710   Oh Aegeus, by this beard and by these legs
    I now embrace, kneeling as a suppliant,
    I implore your pity! Do not see me
    Thrown into exile without home or friend!
    Receive me into your country, allow me
    Into your home! If you do this
    Your dearest wish will by the gods be granted,
    Your house be full of children, yourself die happy!
    You do not know what luck you've chanced on here!
    So potent are the herbs and spells I know
    That I can make you fertile, I can ensure
    That your house will be blessed with children!
AEGEUS. There are many reasons, Medea, why I would like
720   To help you in this way. First to please the gods,
    Then for the promise of children you hold out,
    For in this I had begun to despair.
    This, then, is how it stands with me:
    If ever you reach Athens I will extend
    My hospitality, and give you sanctuary
    As I am bound to do. But I warn you
    I cannot help you leave. If you succeed
    In leaving by yourself and reach my home
    You shall live there in safety. I will not
    Surrender you to anyone. But you must escape

From here without my help. These are my allies.
I've no wish to incur their blame.   730
MEDEA. I will be bound by that. If you will swear
Your oath to this, I shall be well content.
AEGEUS. Why? Don't you trust me? What troubles you?
MEDEA. I trust you, yes. But I have enemies
In Creon, here, and in the house of Pelias.
If you were bound by oath you could not yield me
To either of them if they came for me.
If you make only a promise, not sworn by the gods,
Though you're my friend you might be swayed by them.
I'm weak, while they are rich and powerful.   740
AEGEUS. You show great foresight, Medea. If this
Is what you want I shall not refuse.
An oath will be my safeguard, and my excuse
For holding out against your enemies,
And your case too stands firmer.
So name your gods.
MEDEA. Swear by the earth we walk
And by Helios, my father's father,
And, comprehensively, by all the gods.
AEGEUS. What shall I swear to do, or not to do?
MEDEA. Swear that you will never, of your own will,
Expel me from your country; nor allow   750
While you still live, another to abduct me.
AEGEUS. By Earth I swear this, and by the holy rays
Of the great Sun-god, and all the host of heaven,
I will stand fast to the terms you've made.
MEDEA. That will do well. If you should break this oath
What curse do you invoke upon yourself?
AEGEUS. That fate that always awaits the impious.
MEDEA. Then go in peace, for all is well.
I will come to your city as soon as I may
Once my wishes here have been fulfilled.
CHORUS. May the winged heels of Hermes
Speed you on your way
Safely to your city.   760
And may the gods have pity

29

On your prayers for progeny
For you appear to be
A generous man, Aegeus.
Exit AEGEUS.

MEDEA. Oh Zeus, and your daughter, Justice, and the light
Of Helios the Sun-god! Now, good friends,
I shall triumph over all my enemies!
I shall wreak vengance upon those I hate!
Just where my bark most faltered, this man appears
To offer me safe haven; to him I will make fast
770   The cables of my prow when I have reached
The town and citadel of Athens.
And now I will explain my plans in full.
Do not expect to hear a pleasant story.

I shall send my servant to ask Jason
For one more interview; and when he comes
I shall address him reasonably, saying,
'This pleases me,' and, 'that is good,'
I'll even praise the marriage to the princess
My treacherous lord now celebrates:
'It suits us both,' I'll say.
'It is a clever move.' And then I'll beg him
780   To let my children plead against their exile.
Not that I really mean to leave them here
Exposed to insults in a hostile land,
But so that I can use them cunningly
As messengers of death against the princess.
I'll send them in with gifts to plead with her
Against their banishment; they'll carry
A finely woven robe, and a gold chaplet.
With such dire poisons I shall smear my gifts
That, if she puts them on,
She will die horribly,
And all who touch her.

Enough of her. But my next move
790   I shudder at myself. For I must kill

30

The children I have borne. No one shall stop me.
And when I have quite ruined Jason's house
I'll leave this land, escape all punishment
For this unholy act, my dear sons' murder.
I cannot, will not, tolerate
The scorn of those I hate.

So be it. What use is life to me?
I have no country now, no home, no refuge
From my despair. Oh, I was wrong
To leave my father's house. I never should   800
Have been persuaded by that glib Hellene
Who now, with the gods' help, will pay
A dreadful price. Never again will he see alive
The sons I bore him; nor from his new bride
Breed other heirs, for she must die
An agonising death, slain by my poisons.
Let no one see me as a poor weak woman
Who sits with folded hands. I'm of another mould.
Kind to my friends; implacable to foes.   810
To such as live like me the glory goes.

CHORUS. You have revealed the vengeance you would take.
We must uphold the laws that mortals make.
We ask you to desist, for your own sake.

MEDEA. There is no other way. I can forgive you
For feeling as you do. You are not in my position.

CHORUS. Oh Medea, if you can steel your heart
To slay your sons, you set yourself apart.

MEDEA. To make my husband suffer, I can do it.

CHORUS. And make yourself the sorriest mother alive.

MEDEA. No matter. Every word is a waste of breath
That comes between now and the act.
Nurse! Nurse, you're the only one
I can trust to do it: go in to Jason   820
And bring him here. As you're a woman
And my loyal servant, say nothing of my plans.
Exit NURSE.

CHORUS. The children of Erechtheus, from ancient times,

31

Have basked in the graces of the blessed gods.
They dwell in holy Athens, that unpillaged land,
Feast ever on the glorious food of wisdom.
830 Tread lightly under clear and sparkling skies
Where once the Muses, the nine virgins fair,
Brought forth Harmonia with the golden hair.

The poets sing how Aphrodite drew
Her water from Parnassus' holy spring
And breathed upon this land a gentle breeze,
Balmy and soft; and ever, as she crowns
Her hair with rose-buds, sends her friends,
840 Desire and Love, to sit at Wisdom's side
That Excellence in all be Athens' pride.

How, when it all ends,
Shall the city of sacred waters
Who welcomes her chosen friends
Pollute the air of her daughters
With that of a murderess
850 Fresh from her slaughters?

Consider the act, Medea,
Dwell on the bloody deed.
To kill your sons – the idea
Is heart-rending indeed.
Look, at your knees, in fear
And desperate pity we plead.

860 How will you harden your heart
To kill them? Is it all steel?
Before them, will no tear start
From your eye? And when they kneel
For mercy, how could your hand
The bloody death-stroke deal?
Enter JASON.
JASON. I have come, as you asked. Even though
You hate me bitterly, I'll listen to

32

Whatever new request you have to make.

MEDEA. Jason, I beg your forgiveness for the words I spoke.
We two together once endured much love;
So now you should endure that burst of passion. 870
I have been reasoning with myself.
'Poor foolish heart,' I railed, 'why act so wildly
And set yourself against all good advice?
Why make an enemy of your ruler, Creon,
And of your husband too, who does so wisely
In marrying into a royal house and rearing
Royal brothers for your children?
Should you not curb your temper, when the gods
Seem to be doing all they can to help you?
Consider your children. Have you forgotten 880
That you are fugitives, in need of friends?'

When I had reasoned like this I saw how foolish,
How senseless my rage had been. So now
I must commend your wisdom in creating
This royal alliance for us. I was mad.
I should have shared your plans with you.
Helped you to bring about the match,
Should have been pleased to wait upon the bride.
But we are what we are. I am a woman,
Not evil perhaps, but frail. Men should not 890
Sink to our sorry level, should not use
Our childish weapons to retaliate.
I yield, and must admit that I was wrong,
And have since come to a better understanding.

Come out, children! Come out of the house!
Enter the CHILDREN and TUTOR.
Step out and greet your father with me,
And say goodbye to him. Forget our quarrels
As your mother does: we have made friends again.
Take hold of his hands. Ah me, how sad it is 900
To think what the future hides from us!
Oh, children, your long, long lives stretch out before you

33

As now you stretch your arms out in farewell . . .
Oh dear, how ready with my tears I am today,
How full of fears! Now that I've ended
My quarrel with your father, I can't stop
My tears from falling on your tender heads.

CHORUS. From my eyes too is shaken a fresh tear.
Oh may the gods arrest the evil here!

JASON. This is good, Medea. Not that I blame you
For what you said before. It is quite natural
For a woman to vent her spleen against a husband
910   When he is drawn into another marriage.
But now your heart is turned towards wisdom.
You have chosen the better course at last, and act
Like the sensible woman you are. For you, my sons,
Your father has made good provision: by God's grace,
The time will come when you'll return
And, with your younger brothers,
You'll be the foremost figures in all Corinth.
All you need to do is grow to man's estate.
For all the rest your father, and such gods
As wish us well, are now providing.
920   Grow up, my sons, grow into strong young men
Who will outsoar your father's enemies!
But madam, why do you greet my happy words
With these fresh tears, and sadly turn aside?

MEDEA. It's nothing. I was thinking about the children.

JASON. Take heart then. Their future is provided for.

MEDEA. I will take heart. I do not doubt your word.
Women are weak creatures, given to tears.

JASON. Unhappy woman, why do you grieve
And moan so over these children?

930   MEDEA. I gave them birth. And when you spoke
Of their great future, pity moved in me.
But the reason I wanted further talk with you
Is only told in part. Since it has pleased the King
To banish me from Corinth, I accept
I should not hinder you by staying here.
If I am thought an enemy of Creon, I must go.

But these poor children – let them be reared by you!
Beg Creon not to banish them with me!   940
JASON. I doubt if I can persuade him, but will try.
MEDEA. At least you could ask your wife to plead for them.
JASON. Yes, I will do that, and she'll no doubt agree
  Since she is a woman like the rest of women.
MEDEA. And I can help you here. I'll send
  The children to her with some gifts
  More beautiful than anything yet seen on earth,
  A robe of finest weave, a chaplet of chased gold.
  Go, one of you women, bring the treasure here.   950
  Oh, your princess will be the happiest of women!
  Happy in winning the love of a great hero,
  And in gaining these unique gifts, which Helios
  The sun-god bequeathed to his descendants.
  Now children, take these wedding gifts into your hands
  And take them as offerings to the happy bride.
  No one could turn aside from gifts like these.
JASON. Why do you rob yourself of these great treasures?
  Hers is a royal palace. Golden robes and bands   960
  Are not lacking there. Keep them for yourself.
  If my new wife sets any value on me
  She'll hold me higher than these earthly gifts.
MEDEA. No, let them go. They say that even the gods
  Are swayed by gifts, and for mankind
  Gold is an argument not matched by words.
  Fortune smiles on your bride, and all the gods
  Rejoice at her triumph. She is young and royal.
  While I, to save my sons from exile,
  Would trade my life itself. Now, children,
  When you have gone into the King's rich palace,   970
  Pray to my royal mistress, your father's bride,
  To save you both from exile; offer these treasures
  Into her own hands – this is most important –
  Give these gifts into her hands alone.
  Go quickly now; and if your mission succeeds
  Bring to your mother the news she longs to hear!
  Exit JASON, TUTOR and CHILDREN.

CHORUS. Gone now is every hope,
    All hope that the children might live.
    They are walking toward their doom.
    The hapless bride will take,
    Yes, take up the deadly crown
980   And with her own hands make
    The move that will strike her down.

    She will garland her locks with death,
    And the grace and the sheen divine
    Of the gown will tempt her too,
    She will deck herself as a bride
    To enter the house of the dead.
    From the snare she cannot hide
    And the curse can not be shed.

    And you, Jason, you poor wretch,
990   You've allied yourself with a king
    But it is woe that you have wed.
    You are blind to the fearful fates
    Your sons are walking toward
    And the tortures your bride awaits.
    Woe, Jason, is all your reward.

    And now, O pitiful mother,
    Your sorrows I now bewail.
    You who will kill your children
    To punish your faithless lord
1000   Who deserts his sons and his duty,
    Breaking his god-sworn word,
    For rank, and for youth, and for beauty.
    Enter TUTOR with CHILDREN.

TUTOR. Your children, my lady, are reprieved.
    They will not be exiled. The princess
    Gladly accepted your gifts with her own hands
    And gladly let your children make their peace.
MEDEA. Ah!
TUTOR. Why do you look aside at this good fortune?

Why do you turn your head away
With no welcome for my good news?
MEDEA. Ah!
TUTOR. Your groans don't match the news I bring.
MEDEA. Oh all you gods, have mercy!
TUTOR. Have I without knowing brought bad tidings?
Was I wrong to think my news was good?   1010
MEDEA. Your news is as it is. You are not to blame.
TUTOR. Then why these haunted eyes, these floods of tears?
MEDEA. I have no choice, old friend. The gods and I
In an evil hour devised these things.
TUTOR. Do not despair. In time your sons
Will contrive to bring you home.
MEDEA. Not before I have brought others home . . . Ah!
TUTOR. Be patient. You are not the only mother
To have been parted from her children.
Bear with life patiently, as mortals must.
MEDEA. I will, I will . . . You go into the house now, friend,
And make the day's provision for the children.   1020
Exit TUTOR.
Oh children, children!
You still have a city. You have a home
Where you can tease out your motherless lives
Far, far from me. Far from misery.
While I must go
In exile to an unknown land
Before I have had my joy of you.
Before I have seen you strong and prosperous.
Before I have met your brides
Or decked your bridal beds with banks of blooms
Or lifted high the lovely wedding torch . . .
All that! All that!   1030
Gone by my own hard will.

So it was all in vain.
In vain I reared you, oh my sons,
In vain my loins suffered the spasm and rack
Of your birth, yes, and of your birth.

37

Oh before heaven, the hopes I had of you!
Poor fool.
How you would nurse me gently through old age,
Pay nursing with nursing, and at the end
With loving hands lay out my careless corpse –
A benison we strangely long for.
These fancies now are dead.
Now I must lose you both
Untried in all your duties, and drag out
My useless life in bitterness and sorrow.
No, oh no, never more
Will those fond eyes embrace your mother, no!
A change comes over your lives.

Oh why do you look at me like that
1040   My children, my babies? Why do you smile
That last sweet smile?
Oh what am I to do, what,
What to do? My heart gives way, my heart
Yields to two pairs of smiling eyes!
No. No, I cannot. No. Farewell
To all my schemes, goodbye, go down.
These babies that I bore I'll take away
Far from this land – why wound their father
By wounding them? Why seek
Sorrow in double measure? No.
I will not do it. Farewell
My fiendish schemes.

Yet what am I coming to?
How can I let these enemies of mine
1050   Escape all punishment, live free to mock me?
No, I must face this act.
Oh, oh my craven heart! How could I let
Such weak soft words escape my steely soul?
No! Into the house, children, into the house!
And any here who feels
He has no stomach for my sacrifice

Let him see to it himself, and go.
I shall not falter in my handiwork.

But, oh my heart, do not, do not
Commit my hand to this! Let them go
Oh miserable soul, let these babes go!
Let them live
To cheer you in your empty exile!

No, no, I will not, by all the fiends
Of hell's abyss, I will not, cannot
Hand over my children to be mocked and scorned   1060
By those who hate them. No. They must die.
And I who gave them life
Must take those lives away.
There can be no escape. My course is set.
Already the royal bride has placed my crown
With her own hands about her ivory temples,
Already wrapped the fatal robe about her,
And she is dying, dying.
This I know.

Now, since I have a long sad path to tread,
My sons a longer and a sadder one,
We all must say farewell.
Oh my sons, my babies!
Let me kiss your hands.   1070
Ah, these hands, how I have loved them.
And these lips, these lips, always so dear to me.
Your bodies, your bearing, all so beautiful!
I wish you joy.
Not here, where your father robs you of your rights,
Not now, but in that far, far land . . . Oh come!
Oh yes! those sweet kisses, those soft cheeks,
The fragrant breath of children,
My children!
No. Go. I cannot
I cannot look on you a moment longer.

I cannot bear this pain.
The CHILDREN go in.
Now it is here. Now I embrace
The nature of the awful act I face.
1080   But rage, that fuels the foulest deeds of man,
Rage masters all, as conscience never can.

CHORUS. Subtler and graver issues than men think fit
For women to pursue I've often probed.
For we too have a Muse that lives in us
And draws us towards wisdom. Not all, perhaps,
But in any crowd of women there's a section
Who aren't incapable of sage reflection.

1090   My Muse asserts that mortals without children
Are happier by far than any parent.
A childless couple cannot ever know
Whether or not the rearing up of children
Is a blessing or a curse; in fact, of course
They've spared themselves a host of ills, or worse.

But those who house the sweet race of the young
I watch being worn to shreds throughout their lives.
First trying to train them in the ways of virtue,
1100   Then struggling to provide well for their future;
And through all this one question drives them mad:
Are they toiling for good children, or for bad?

But worst of all a parent's griefs is this;
Suppose they've found sufficient means to live
And seen their children safely through to manhood,
Free from bad company and other vices;
Still Fate may come to strike the children dead
1110   And bear them off to Hades. Why do the gods
On mortal man this final grief impose,
The pain of children lost, the worst of woes.

MEDEA. My friends, I have been waiting a long time
To hear what may have happened inside the palace
And now I see a slave of Jason's coming,

40

Gasping for breath. He must bring urgent news. 1120
Enter MESSENGER.
MESSENGER. Fly, fly, Medea! this appalling thing you've done
  Is against every law of man! Take any route,
  By sea or land, you must escape at once.
MEDEA. Why, what has happened to call for such a flight?
MESSENGER. Only a moment ago the princess died,
  And Creon her father too, slain by your poison.
MEDEA. The best news you could bring! I'll count you
  From now on amongst my friends and benefactors.
MESSENGER. What? Are you sane? To hear such news
  With joy, and without fear – your mind 1130
  Must be deranged.
MEDEA. There are words I could say
  To answer what you say.
  But let us take our time, my friend.
  I want to hear the manner of their death.
  It would be a double joy indeed
  For me to hear that they died hideously.
MESSENGER. When the two children,
  The fruit of your womb,
  Came into the palace
  Slaves who had shared your
  Griefs were all joyful.
  Rumour spread quickly:
  The quarrel was ended
  Between you and your lord. 1140
  One kissed your children's hands and one their curly hair.
  While I for joy went with them to the princess.

  The mistress we now loved
  As once we loved you
  Only had eyes for Jason
  Before she saw the children;
  Then she dropped her eyes
  And turned her face away
  In anger at their coming.
  To check his young bride's wrath 1150

41

Jason then argued:
Do not be angry with friends; turn back to us;
Those whom I love, you must accept as friends.
Take up these offered gifts and beseech your father
That he revoke these children's banishment.

As soon as she saw the gifts
She held back no longer
But went to her father's chamber
And did as her husband asked.
Then almost before Jason
And his sons had left the palace
She took up and wrapped about her
The finely embroidered gown.
1160 She set the golden chaplet
About her brow, arranging
Her tresses at the bright mirror,
Smiling at her reflection.
Then rising from her seat on delicate feet she tripped
Lightly across the chamber, all the time exulting
In the way the radiant robe fell from her ankle.

When suddenly a scene
Of horror came upon us!
She paled, staggered backwards
Trembling in every limb,
Then sank into a seat
1170 To save herself from falling.
An old woman slave of hers
Thought it a fit from Pan
And raised the cry of prayer,
But then she saw the girl's mouth flecked with white foam,
And her eyes roll in their sockets, all the blood
Drain from her face; then the old woman raised
A scream far different from her former prayer.

One maid ran for the King,
Another to tell Jason

Of his bride's sudden sickness.
The palace echoed with running.   1180
For as long as a swift walker
Might take to circle the palace
She lay in a speechless swoon;
Then with a fearful shriek
She came to with open eyes
To grapple with twin tortures:
A stream of ravening flame shot from her golden crown;
The gown the children gave her consumed her fair white

flesh.

She leapt up, all ablaze, violently shook her head   1190
To cast off her burning crown, but it held firm
And, as her tresses swirled, blazed with redoubled fury.

Then to the ground she sank
Exhausted by the battle,
Past recognition now
Save by a father's eyes;
Her own eyes blind and gone,
Her face unnatural,
And from her head a stream
Of mingled blood and fire
Ran down; and all her flesh,
Gnawed by those secret poisons,
Like tears of pitch from a pine tree, melted from off her

bones,   1200

A sight most horrible. Not one of us would dare
Touch the tortured body; we'd been warned by what we'd

seen.

Suddenly in came her father,
Ignorant of how she'd died,
And fell upon the corpse,
Folding his arms about her,
Kissing her and crying,
Crying aloud and saying:
'Oh my poor dear daughter, which of the gods destroyed you

43

In such a foul, foul manner? Who is it robs me of you,
Ripe as I am for death? Oh my poor child, alas,
1210   I wish I could die with you!'

His lamentations over
The old man would have risen
But found himself held fast
By the finespun robe which clung
As ivy clings to the baytree.
A terrible struggle followed.
He tried and tried to rise.
She always held him back.
And when he pulled with all his might his flesh
Tore from his aged bones. Soon he struggled no more.
Pain overcame him. Gasping, he sank into death.

So there they lie: daughter
1220   And aged father, side by side,
A sight to call forth tears.
And as for you, Medea,
I cannot think about you.
Make good your own escape.

Again I find myself thinking
That human life is a shadow.
Yes, and without shrinking
Will say the pursuit of wisdom,
That juggling with thoughts and words,
Is folly, nothing but folly.
No mortal man is happy; should fate bestow
More wealth on him than's common, even so,
1230   He may be prosperous; but happy, no!
  CHORUS. This day the gods will heap, it seems,
    On Jason's back a load of woes.
    And Creon's child, we weep for you.
    Your soul, as Jason's payment, goes
    To Hades' halls, far from our view.
  MEDEA. Friends, my resolve is firm.

44

I will kill my children now,
Then leave this land.
Not a moment's delay, in case
Some revenging butcher
Gets to them before me.
They must die in any case
And since they must   1240
Let it be me that kills them,
Me, the mother that bore them!

Steel yourself, you, my heart, you must hold firm.
The deed is dreadful but it must be done.
Come, take up the sword, you wretched hand,
Take it, and move toward that dark frontier
Where your life of sorrows begins. No cowardice, now,
No thoughts about how dear your children are,
Or how you are their mother. This one brief day
Forget your love for them; grieve for them later.
For though you will kill them, they were still your

                                   darlings . . .
I am a woman of sorrows.   1250

CHORUS. Oh Earth, look up! Oh Sun, whose rays
  Peer into everything, look down
  On this lost woman here, before she stains
  Her murderous hands with her own children's blood!
  They are your scions, by your own kin bred:
  The blood of gods should not by man be shed.

  Oh light of Zeus, stay her hand,
  Hold back this demon-driven fiend   1260
  And drive her from this house. The throes
  Of childbirth wasted, wasted all your care
  Of those sweet babes, oh you who came
  Safe through a host of hazards to this shame!

  Oh miserable woman, why must rage
  Consume your heart, allowing murder in?

For when the blood of kin spills on the ground
The gods hold it pollution and revenge
Themselves on mortal man, and for each crime
1270 The killer's house will surely pay in time.

CHILD 1 (*in*). Oh help, help! Where can I go
To escape my mother's blow?

CHILD 2 (*in*). We're lost, dear brother, that I know!

CHORUS. Oh listen, listen,
The children cry out!
Oh woman of sorrow!
Oh victim of fate!
Shall I enter the house
For the children's sake?
Could I stop this foul murder?

CHILD 1 (*in*). Oh help, by heaven I pray!
Send help to keep her sword away!

CHILD 2 (*in*). Too late! The sword is on us now . . .

CHORUS. Oh miserable mother, surely your heart
Is made of steel, or flinty stone
1280 To slay like this the offspring of your womb!
Of all the wives of old that I have heard
I know of only one who killed her children.
Ino, it was, by the gods driven mad
When Zeus' wife had hounded her from home
To wander in the world. But she, poor waif,
Paid for her crime by her own hand. She leapt
Over the wave—torn cliff, where the sea runs,
United then in death with her slain sons.

Can there be any horrors worse than this
1290 For fate to send us? Oh the calamities
The passions of women bring to the lives of men!

JASON. Women of Corinth, gathered here in the courtyard,
Is that foul murderess still inside the house
Or has she fled already? She'd have to hide
Beneath the earth, or soar on wings
Into the vaults of heaven to escape
The vengeance of the royal house of Corinth!

Does she expect to go unpunished
When she has killed the rulers of this land?   1300
Enough of her. Those she has wronged
Will deal with her. I am here to save my sons,
In case the family of the king should kill them
In revenge for their mother's crime.

CHORUS. Poor Jason, you would never use such words
  If you knew how far your misery extends.

JASON. What misery? Can she want to kill me too?

CHORUS. Your sons are dead, by their own mother's hand.

JASON. What? What are you saying? My sons dead?
  Woman, you have killed me too.   1310

CHORUS. Your children are both dead. Be sure of that.

JASON. Where did she kill them? Here inside the palace?

CHORUS. Have the doors opened; you will see them dead.

JASON. Quickly, you men, unbar these doors!
  Let me see these two horrors – my dead sons,
  And the woman I mean to kill.
  MEDEA in mid-air, on a chariot drawn
  by dragons, her CHILDREN's corpses by her.

MEDEA. Why do you batter on those doors?
  To find the dead, and me, their murderer?
  Don't waste your time. If you have anything
  To say to me, then say it if you must
  But you will never lay a hand on me.   1320
  The chariot that the Sun, my father's father,
  Has sent to save me is too swift for you.

JASON. You thrice-damned woman! Loathed by the gods
  As no woman ever was, and loathed by me,
  Yes, and by all mankind, who raised a sword
  To pierce the tender hearts of her own sons
  Leaving me childless and destroyed!
  You have done this, and still outstare
  The Earth and Sun, having polluted them!
  May the gods rain curses on you!

  I see now what I missed on that black day
  When I brought you, doomed, from your barbarian home

47

To live in Hellas, a traitor to your father
1330 And to the land that nurtured you.
The gods have hurled on me the gathered curses
That you have earned, you who had killed your brother
Before you ever stepped aboard the 'Argo',
Launching your fleet of crimes.
Then you wed me and, having borne me sons,
Out of your lust and jealousy, you killed them.

Not one woman in all Hellas could have done it.
1340 Yet I, disdaining them, chose to wed you,
A carrier of doom; not a woman
But a lioness far fiercer than that Scylla
Who guards the Tyrrhenian Sea.
But I know I cannot wound with a thousand words
A nature as brazen as yours. Go, then,
You evil witch, you child-killer,
Leave me to mourn my fate.
I shall never enjoy my new-found bride,
Nor know my sons, whom I have loved and reared,
Nor even hear them say a last farewell.
1350 All, all is lost to me.
MEDEA. I could make a long retort to such a speech,
But Zeus, our Father, knows what I did for you
And how you then repaid me.
The gods did not ordain that you should scorn me
And lead a joyous life that mocked my love,
Nor was your royal bride, nor Creon her father,
To thrust me from their land and go unpunished.
So, if you like, call me a lioness,
Worse than a Tuscan Scylla: I have reached
1360 Your heart, as I had planned.
JASON. You are grieved too: you share my pain.
MEDEA. You can be sure of that; but it relieves my pain
To know you cannot mock me.
JASON. Oh my children, you have a vile mother!
MEDEA. My sons, your father's lust brought on your ruin.
JASON. It was not my hand that killed them.

MEDEA. No, it was your heedless insult to me
  In making your new marriage.

JASON. You think a second marriage reason enough
  To kill your children?

MEDEA. You think a woman should think nothing of it?

JASON. A modest woman, yes. But you see everything as evil
                                                      now.

MEDEA. Your sons are dead. Let it pierce your heart: 1370
  Your sons are dead!

JASON. No. My sons live on, to bring a curse on you.

MEDEA. The gods know well who started this trail of sin.

JASON. Indeed, they know that hate-filled heart of yours.

MEDEA. Yours is as full of hate; I'm weary
  Of listening to your bitter tongue.

JASON. And I of hearing yours. That makes
  The terms of parting easy.

MEDEA. What terms? What do you want?
  I am as ready to go as you to have me gone.

JASON. Give me the children's bodies, to bury and mourn.

MEDEA. No, never! I will bury them myself.
  I will carry them to Hera's sacred field
  Above the restless sea, where our enemies
  Would never dare to violate their tombs,   1380
  [And in this land of Corinth I'll ordain
  A solemn feast and annual sacrifice
  In meek atonement for this godless murder.]
  Now I shall go to live in peace in Athens.
  The oaths that Aegeus swore will be my shield.
  But you, as you deserve, will die
  Not like a hero, but like any slave,
  Crushed by a falling timber
  From your rotting ship the 'Argo'
  As you sleep under her shadow
  Nursing your bitter memories of our love
  To your wretched, bitter end.

JASON. The curse of our children's blood
  And their avenging spirits follow you!   1390

MEDEA. What god listens to a breaker of oaths,

A breaker of every law of hospitality?

JASON. You damnable witch! Murderer of children!

MEDEA. Go into your house. Go and bury your wife.

JASON. I am going. I have lost my sons.

MEDEA. You have not yet felt true grief, but that will come:
Wait until old age is with you too.

JASON. Oh my dear, dear children.

MEDEA. Dear to their mother, not to you.

JASON. And yet you killed them?

MEDEA. Yes: to break your heart.

1400 JASON. Let me give them one last fond kiss.

MEDEA. You want to embrace them now! You,
Who would have seen them driven into exile!

JASON. By heaven, I beg you! Let me touch their gentle bodies!

MEDEA. No, no. Your words are lost on the wind.

JASON. Oh Zeus, do you see this?
See how I am driven away,
How I am wronged by this lioness,
This murderer of children?

Yet as I can and may
I'll mourn them solemnly.

1410 I call the gods to witness
That having slain my sons
You would not even let me
Give them one last embrace
Or bury them. The days were ill
When I begot these sons for you to kill.

CHORUS. Zeus, from his Olympian throne,
To man dispenses many a fate.
Often he brings about a state
Of things we could not have expected.
The ends we looked for, god rejected.
As this sad tale will illustrate.

THE PHOENICIAN WOMEN

Translated by David Thompson

Characters

JOCASTA, *formerly Queen of Thebes*
ANTIGONE, *her daughter*
TUTOR *to Antigone*
CHORUS *of women from Phoenicia*
POLYNEICES, *younger son of Jocasta*
ETEOCLES, *elder son of Jocasta, now King of Thebes*
CREON, *brother of Jocasta*
TEIRESIAS, *a blind prophet*
MENOECEUS, *son of Creon*
FIRST MESSENGER
SECOND MESSENGER
OEDIPUS

A shortened version of this translation was originally written for performance by students at the Royal Academy of Dramatic Art in the Spring term, 1967. Re-titled 'The Sons of Oedipus', it was broadcast on BBC Radio 3, on 29 July 1976, with Siobhan McKenna as Jocasta and Michael Redgrave as Oedipus, directed by John Theocharis. Its first public stage performance was given at the Greenwich Theatre, on 3 February 1977 with the following cast:

JOCASTA	Siobhan McKenna
NARRATOR/CHORUS	Freda Dowie
ANTIGONE	Ursula Mohan
TUTOR	Patrick Hannaway
POLYNEICES	Scott Antony
ETEOCLES	Michael Deacon
CREON	Ewan Hooper
TEIRESIAS	Richard Mayes
MENOECEUS	Jonathan Warren
FIRST MESSENGER	David Brierley
SECOND MESSENGER	Frank Barrie
OEDIPUS	Denys Hawthorne

Designed by Bruno Santini
Directed by David Thompson

Scene One
Prologue.

JOCASTA. Curse on you, light of day!
    You cut your way through the stars,
    Your sun-car flashing gold, your headlong horses
    Scattering fire across our sky!
    But on that distant day
    You hung over Thebes like a doom,
    Like an omen,
    When Cadmus, from his far Phoenician shore,
    Found his way here . . .

    Cadmus it was who wed Aphrodite's daughter,
    And they had Polydorus: he in turn
    (So history tells) sired Labdacus, and he
    Was the father of Laius. Laius the King
    Was my husband. I am Menoeceus' daughter,   10
    The sister of Creon. I am Jocasta . . .

    Barren and empty – with Laius my marriage
    For years was barren, for years the house was empty.
    He went to the oracle, questioned the god,
    Begged that our union be blessed with issue.
    He had his answer –
    'Lord of Thebes and its famed horses,
    Sow not that seed. The gods have ruled against it.
    If you father a child, that child will kill you
    And all your house go down in blood.'   20
    But lust had its way, lust and wine,
    And Laius got me with child.
    He knew he had offended,
    He remembered that the god had warned him,
    And he took the babe and gave it to herdsmen
    To abandon on the high slopes of Cithaeron.

But first, to tether it, he spiked its ankles
With an iron skewer. That's how it got its name.
The child was later known as 'swollen foot',
And that in Greece is – OEDIPUS.

But horse–tenders from across the border,
Ranging the hills, discovered it,
And took it home, and gave it to their queen.
30 She suckled the babe I laboured for, persuaded
Her husband it was hers. And so my son grew up.
Perhaps he guessed something. Perhaps he heard the story.
But with the first flush of his young beard upon him
He was fretting to know more – who were his parents?
He set out for the oracle of Phoebus,
And so, for the second time, did Laius,
My husband Laius, needing to be reassured
The child he had exposed no longer lived.
They met, the two of them,
Met at the crossroads on the way to Phocis.
Laius' driver ordered the stranger out of his way,
40 'Stand aside for the King there!' –
But Oedipus came on. Never answered.
Not to be demeaned.
And the horses jibbed, reared,
Hooves hit his heel, that heel, drew blood . . .
Oh, what does the telling matter?
There is only the outcome, the catastrophe.
Son slew his father –
And he took the chariot home and
Gave it to him who was, he thought, his father . . .

It was after that the Sphinx came, terrorising Thebes,
Plundering her people, when they no longer
Had a king, their queen no husband.
So Creon my brother had heralds give it out
That he who could read the Sphinx's riddle should have me.
50 And who was it mastered that she-devil's rhyme
But my son Oedipus,

And was rewarded with all honour and power
And crowned King of Thebes,
And married her who bore him,
Never knowing, poor wretch,
As she never knew herself, a mother
Coupling with her child . . .
So to my son I bore sons,
Eteocles and my fine, my famous Polyneices.
And two girls – Ismene whom her father named,
And the elder named Antigone by me.
But when he learned the truth,
Knew his marriage-bed was where he had been born,
Knew he was the root and heart of all disaster,   60
He tried to tear the horror from himself,
Searching in the sockets of his eyes with needles
Till they burst blood . . .

They locked him away, my sons, when they were grown,
Shuffled him out of sight to try and forget,
Try and quiet the questions that troubled conscience.
But Oedipus lives on, in the house here,
His grief grown cancerous within him,
And always he curses his sons
So that they shrink with the terror of it –
'Inherit my house? No, inherit from me
The sword and the sword's edge. Share that between you!'
Even a blasphemy is heard in heaven.
If they stayed together, the gods might heed it.   70
So they made a pact, that first Polyneices,
Being the younger, agree to leave Thebes
While his brother remain and rule – each year to change.
But once secure, once in power, Eteocles
Would not be thrust from his throne.
Polyneices was banished. He went to Argos
And won himself there a royal bride.
Now, with the might of Argos mustered behind him,
He has come again, marching against us,
Claiming his father's throne and what is owed him.   80

I shall try to undo their quarrel. I have persuaded
Son to meet son under letters of truce
Before battle flares. And he'll come.
My messenger brings me word that he'll come.
O Zeus, hidden from us in the brightness of heaven,
You who are all-powerful, all-wise, you cannot
Forever deny all blessing to one poor mortal.
Save us, O Zeus! Hear my prayer.
Grant that my sons be reconciled . . .

Scene Two
The Watchers on the Roof

TUTOR. Highness, are you there? Fair flower of Oedipus' house
That you are, your mother has given permission, Antigone –
90   She has said you may leave your maiden chamber
To go up on the roof, to the very top,
So you can see the Argive army
Just as you asked. But wait now, wait! First
I must reconnoitre. I want no townsfolk
Meeting us out in the street and gossiping.
What they say doesn't matter to me, I'm a servant,
But you – are a princess. Oh, I've so much to tell you
About meeting your brother, taking
The Queen your mother's offer of truce to him,
The things I saw in the Argive camp, and heard . . .
100   Good, there's no one about. We'll try the old stairs
Of cedar wood. Watch where you're putting your feet.
The view from up here takes in the whole plain
And along by the river as far as the spring of Dirce.
You'll get an idea how vast their army is.
ANTIGONE. Please give me your hand, I need your hand . . .
TUTOR. Youth calls on age, does it?
ANTIGONE. It's steep up the last step . . .
TUTOR. Here, take hold, lass – up you come!
Just in time too. It's starting to move.
The army's on the move. It's splitting up
Into battalions . . .

ANTIGONE. O Artemis, protect us! The whole wide plain   110
Is flashing bronze!

TUTOR. Oh, yes. Your brother
Didn't mean us to be unimpressed,
Bringing such ranks of horse and infantry
Against us.

ANTIGONE. Can our gates hold them? Are the brazen bolts
Secure? The old stone walls?

TUTOR. Never fear. Inside the city all's safe.
Now mark that first man, remember him well.

ANTIGONE. The one with the white crest out in front?   120
So, who is he? He carries that great bronze shield
As if it weighed nothing.

TUTOR. A famous captain, my lady.

ANTIGONE. Where from? What's his name?

TUTOR. He comes from Mycenae. A proud family.
They have lands along the river Lerna.
He's the Lord Hippomedon.

ANTIGONE. Oh, he looks arrogant.
He frightens me, like those giants in pictures
Who stand on mountaintops and throw thunderbolts.
As though he weren't human.   130

TUTOR. Do you see the one crossing the river?

ANTIGONE. The foreign one with that strange armour?
Who is he?

TUTOR. Tydeus.

ANTIGONE. Tydeus? Who became brother to my brother,
To my Polyneices, when they married sisters?
He looks so – different. He's armed like some
Wild tribesman.

TUTOR. He's from Aetolia, child.
They all carry target-shields like that,
And those throwing-spears. They're deadly marksmen.   140

ANTIGONE. You know so much about them. Where
Did you learn it all?

TUTOR. In their camp,
When I met your brother. I learned their ensigns.

ANTIGONE. But who's that skirting the Zetheus monument,

With the flowing hair and fierce eyes? He's so young
To command them. But look how the soldiers
Press at his heels and throng about him.

150 TUTOR. That's Parthenopaeus, Atalanta's son.

ANTIGONE. May Artemis, who hunts the hills with his mother,
Shoot him down like a wild beast for coming
To lay waste my city!

TUTOR. I pray so too, child.
Yet the cause that brings them is not unjust,
And the gods may see that. That's my fear.

ANTIGONE. Where's he
Who was born to such pain, to so many troubles,
Who shares one mother with me? Dear tutor,
Dear, dear tutor, point me out Polyneices.

TUTOR. Over there, near the tomb to Niobe's daughters.
160 He stands at Adrastus' side. Can you see him?

ANTIGONE. Yes, I see. Not clearly, but I can see
A remembered shape, the hint of him.
Oh, could I fly to him, race down the wind to him,
To my own dear brother, and fling my arms
Round his neck, and kiss away all that time
Of exile and suffering. Isn't he glorious
In his golden war-gear? He dazzles like the sun
In the morning!

170 TUTOR. He'll be here soon. The truce
Will bring him. Your heart won't be empty long.

ANTIGONE. And who is that one, driving the chariot
With white horses?

TUTOR. That is the priest-king, Amphiaraos,
Bringing the animals for sacrifice, with which
To appease this land.

ANTIGONE. He reminds me somehow
Of the full moon, sailing high, shedding
Her mellow light. He rides on so serenely.
But where's the one who's always shouting
180 Terrible threats and taunting us? Where's Capaneus?

TUTOR. Down there, below, at the foot of the bastion,
Busy gauging how high the walls are, and if

They're built so he could scale them.

ANTIGONE. O Nemesis, you know the way to smother,
A man's boasting. One bolt from Zeus,
One lightning-flash of his wrath, and that mouth
Would be stopped for ever. Didn't he promise
His prize would be the daughters of Thebes
To take home and give to the wives of Mycenae –
That he'd net us like birds and give us away
As bondslaves? Never, oh never, never, great   190
Goddess of us who bear children, I beg you,
Golden-haired daughter of Zeus, subject us to slavery!

TUTOR. Come, child, come now, it's time to go in.
Let us go down again, back to your room
Where it's quiet and safe. You've got what you asked for,
Seen what you came to see. Crowds are gathering.
The town is troubled, and womenfolk press
Round the palace. Save me from censuring tongues
If one of them sees you! They'll turn it into a scandal.   200
Oh, why must women so love speaking ill of each other?

CHORAL ODE I

Far away left far behind now
the city I set sail from.
I bade farewell to Tyre and the sea-swell
greeted me,
carried me from my Phoenician shore.
Apollo called me, they were sending me
to serve him –
was I not chosen, favoured, singled out
Phoenicia's gift to him
to serve him at his Delphic shrine
below the snow-topped peaks of Parnassus?
And swift oars sped me
up the Ionian Sea past
the unharvestable deeps off Sicily,   210
while wild winds roared out of the west
with heavenly clamour
like chariots racing . . .

And I came to Cadmus' land –
I who was chosen for Apollo
beauty's prize of all my city,
came here to Thebes which Cadmus founded
Cadmus the son of Agenor . . .
I who am also of the race of Agenor
here to the towered town of his famous sons.
But I should be now in Apollo's service
adorning his temple

220   clad all in gold like the statues there –
Delphi still waits for me
to dip my hair in its sacred spring
in dedication . . .

O sacred Rock I long for you, flaming
with fire double-tongued above Delphi,
the dance of Dionysus on the heights!
And you yielding – o miracle of the vine –

230   your one ripe swelling cluster
day by day renewed
for Dionysus!
Holiest of holies I long for you,
cave of the dragon!
You mountain watch-towers of the gods themselves,
and you, Parnassus-peak snowmantled,
god-haunted!
Would that I too were treading
that deathless dance,
would that I too
were where Apollo dwells
at the hollow mid-point of the world,
and I were far from here,
and this dread taken from me . . .

For now there's War himself

240   marching against us – look!
parading before the walls.
Can you feel it, the lust for battle

rising . . .?
This is a time of blood and fire.
Oh save this city!
We cling together
one love one fear
one nation in mourning.
If this dear land of tall towers
should suffer –
one blood one race
descended all
from the horn'd moon-maiden Io,
we share one agony . . .

Thick now as thunderclouds   250
the war-shields surge and settle round the town.
It's the signal for red battle.
You wait for that don't you, War God?
It's you brings the Furies' curse
on the sons of Oedipus . . .
Oh I dread the power of Argos
and what heaven will do.
There's a man on his way here now,
armed – look! a man finding his way home,   260
and the gods know what his quarrel is
and they know it is not unjust . . .

Scene Three
The Meeting of Two Brothers

POLYNEICES. The warders slipped the bolts and let me through.
 No trouble. So, inside the walls. Now
 Is the time to fear. They have me in their net
 And I may not get out again unbloodied.
 Be wary. Watch for the trap. This side, that side.
 Sword drawn and eager. Let no man tempt it!
 Who's there?
 Or was it a noise scared me? Set foot   270
 Once on enemy soil and each thing

Threatens you, whatever you dare.
My mother persuaded me to this,
This coming here under truce. Well, I trust her.
Or do I trust her? Ah, here's sanctuary . . .
An altar. And women in front of the palace.
So. Back in its blind scabbard goes my sword.
I'll ask who they are. Strangers – I see you *are* strangers –
Where are you from? What do you do in Greece?

280   CHORUS. We are Phoenicians, sir – sent to serve
At Apollo's shrine, but caught here on our way
When Argos marched against Thebes. And you –
Who may you be, venturing here?

POLYNEICES. I am known to the people of Thebes. My father,
Oedipus the son of Laius: my mother,

290   The Queen Jocasta. I am Polyneices.

CHORUS. O my lord, you have come,
You who are kin to the sons of Agenor
Who sent me . . .
Master, let me fall on my knees before you,
Let me give thanks and honour you
After the custom of my people.
At last you have come to your own land again!
Queen Jocasta, come out, come out!
Open the gates!
Mother of him who has come again,
Can you not hear us?
Oh, why do you tarry within there
And not come out

300   And wind your son in your arms!

JOCASTA. I hear you. I can hear your foreign babbling.
I come. Old, slow and unsteady, but I come.
O my son . . .
At last. After such uncountable days
To look on you. Embrace your mother.
Hold me close, close . . .
Oh, the touch of you . . .
Lean down, let me feel your face,
Let me feel the dark curls nestle at my neck,

Overshadow me . . .
Oh, my darling, past hope, past dreaming of . . .   310
My son in my arms . . .
What words are there? How shall I grasp it all,
Hold on to such happiness,
Each shift and shade of it, so precious . . .
How can hand, tongue . . .
It dances with me so, to and fro . . .
I had almost forgotten . . .
You left your home so empty.
Yes, I know, you were driven away,
Your brother abused you,
But those you loved longed for you,   320
Thebes itself longed for you.
I cut my hair and wept,
Gave myself up to grief –
The white I once wore, child,
Is not for me now.
I dress in rags now,
Rags and black night.
And the old, blind man in the house here,
Since the pair of you broke away,
Has only his pain and one longing he clings to,   330
How he can kill himself,
Swift sword or a rope in the dark roof,
And curses himself for cursing his sons,
And cries out, and weeps,
And hides in his darkness.
But you, son – is it true what they tell me?
That you're married? That you've pledged yourself,
Pledged the name of your children, to foreigners   340
And foreign ways? Oh no, that was wrong.
It wrongs me, your mother, and it wrongs
The memory of Laius, a marriage like that
Far, far from home. What good can that come to?
A happy mother should raise the marriage-torch
At her son's wedding. But I was not there.
The waters of Ismenus never ran for your anointing,

There was no singing in Thebes to bring your bride home . . .
350 It's all wrong, wrong. O God, put an end to it!
This fighting, this jealousy and hate,
Your father's guilt – is that the cause?
This madness that riots through our house
Like drunken devils –
I suffer for all of it, all the pain of it
Gathers upon me.

CHORUS. From the terror of birth to the terror of losing,
A mother's care
Clings to her child. So, always.

POLYNEICES. Mother, what brought me here?
Why have I come, in my right mind and yet
Without thinking, here where my enemies are?
It's because we can't help ourselves. There's a
Yearning for home compels every one of us –
And those who say anything else do not know,
360 They're toying with words. I was frightened to come,
Frightened of treachery and of my brother,
Frightened of death. I came through my city
With drawn sword and eyes all around me.
One thing kept me going – my trust in you
And the truce you made to draw me inside these walls.
But I came full of tears, after all this time
Seeing the houses again, the altars,
The schoolrooms where I spent my boyhood,
The river Dirce – all I have been cheated of
And driven away from, to live in a city
370 Which would never be mine, and waste my years weeping.
And yet what is past grief to this grief – to see you
With shaved head and black dress of mourning?
O God, have pity on me!
How terrible is hatred, mother, between those
Who belong together. How hard the healing of it.
What does my father do now, here in his palace,
He who sees darkness? What of my sisters?
Do they feel for me in my exile's misery?

JOCASTA. There's surely a god destroying us, one by one.

And I was the start of it. I bore what was   380
Forbidden. Married your father and had you.
But what of that now? The gods dispose
And we must bear it. Yet I yearn to know –
But I fear to ask, I fear its hurt . . .

POLYNEICES. Ask what you will, mother. Do not
  Leave it unsaid. Your wish is my wish.

JOCASTA. It haunts me what exile has been to you.

POLYNEICES. Hard to bear. Hardest of all things.
  A cruel word and a crueller fate.

JOCASTA. In what most cruel?   390

POLYNEICES. You are never a free man. The tongue is fettered.

JOCASTA. A man can utter his thought. He's not a slave.

POLYNEICES. Ah, but we serve masters. We're subject
  To their whim, dependent on them.

JOCASTA. If they're fools, you must suffer them?

POLYNEICES. Exiles are beggars, and to gain their ends,
  Despite themselves, must ape the slave's style.

JOCASTA. They say that exiles always have hope to feed on.

POLYNEICES. Hope has bright eyes to see the future, yes.
  It keeps you waiting, though. Waiting for ever!

JOCASTA. Then does not time prove that hope is empty?

POLYNEICES. Perhaps. And yet when everything is black
  It has a kind of beauty.

JOCASTA. Later you married. That kept you fed.   400
  What fed you before that?

POLYNEICES. Sometimes I ate, sometimes I fasted.
  I lived from day to day.

JOCASTA. But your father had friends – didn't they help you?

POLYNEICES. Look for friends when you prosper. You have
                                none when you don't.

JOCASTA. You're of royal blood. Did that give you no standing?

POLYNEICES. How could it do so? I am dispossessed.
  My birth never won me a crust of bread!

JOCASTA. It does seem true there's nowhere men can trust
  But their own dear land, their home.

POLYNEICES. Words can't express how much it means.

JOCASTA. But you went to Argos. How, my son? Why?

POLYNEICES. Why? I don't know. Some god, was it,
  Called me there? Fate?
JOCASTA. In all things there's some divine purpose. You found
                                   there
  A bride. How was that?
POLYNEICES. Adrastus heard an oracle.
410 JOCASTA. 'Heard an oracle'? What do you mean?
POLYNEICES. 'Marry your daughters,' it said, 'to the boar and
                                 the lion.'
JOCASTA. What have wild brutes' names to do with you?
POLYNEICES. It was night when I knocked at Adrastus' gate . . .
JOCASTA. Looking for a bed, poor wandering one?
POLYNEICES. Yes. But then there arrived a second refugee.
JOCASTA. In as awful plight as you were? Who was he?
POLYNEICES. Tydeus, son of Oeneus.
420 JOCASTA. But why did you seem to Adrastus like wild beasts?
POLYNEICES. We'd fought over a mattress. Like two beasts.
JOCASTA. He was reminded of the oracle . . .?
POLYNEICES. And gave us two his two young daughters.
JOCASTA. Have they brought you happiness, these marriages?
POLYNEICES. We have blameless wives. They still content us.
JOCASTA. Now you have rallied an army to your cause.
  What made them follow you here?
POLYNEICES. The King Adrastus has sworn to restore
  Both his two sons-in-law, Tydeus and me,
  Each to his own home. I am the first.
  They are all here to help me –
430   From Mycenae, from Argos, mighty men all –
  Help which I hate but I need.
  This is Thebes, my Thebes, I march against . . .
  Do you hear me, gods? It was never my will
  That spear of mine should be levelled
  Against those that raised me, those I love.
  Mother, we look to you. You are the only one
  To unravel this web of disaster,
  To knit us in love again, as we were born,
  And rescue us all – me, you, this city.
440   Haven't they always said, what belongs to a man

Is what wins him honour? And possession is power?
I say so too. That's why I am here,
To reclaim my own. What use is birth to a beggar?
CHORUS. Look, look, the meeting is made up. Here now
  Comes Eteocles. Jocasta, it rests with you.
  You are the mother of these two.
  Have you the words to reconcile them?
ETEOCLES. Yes, mother? You called. I am here. I come for your
                                                 sake.
  What do we have to do? Will someone begin?
  Come, the city's defences wait on me.
  I have interrupted my preparations
  To hear what you had to say. Wasn't that why   450
  You prevailed on me to let this creature
  Enter our walls?
JOCASTA. Stop, Eteocles, stop it. You cannot be hasty
  And be just. Slow words for wisdom's sake.
  Check that impatience in your heart, that anger
  In your eye. What do you think you see?
  Medusa's head? This is your brother.
  Your brother come again. You too, Polyneices.
  Turn and face him. How can you speak to him
  Or listen to him if you will not look at him?
  I wish to advise you wisely, both of you.   460
  When friends who have quarrelled come together,
  Meet face to face, they have to think
  Of one thing only – what they came for.
  Nothing else. The past and past wrongs
  Must have no place in their remembrance.
  Son Polyneices, you shall speak first.
  You have come here at the head of an Argive army
  Claiming you suffer injustice. Now God
  Be our judge and settle this strife for us.
POLYNEICES. Truth is so simple. A just cause
  Needs no devious defence. It argues   470
  Its own rightness. It is the wrong
  Which is so sickly weak it can't stand up
  Without the help of dubious doctoring.

I cared for the future of my father's house.
It was in both our interests – mine and my brother's.
I wanted to escape the fate that Oedipus
Had cursed us with, and voluntarily
I left this land and I surrendered
To this man here the kingship of it
For a year's cycle, so that in turn
I might myself resume it, and not
Involve us both in hatred and violence,
480   Doing and suffering harm.
But that is what happened.
He agreed with the idea, he swore an oath
Before the gods, but then did nothing he promised.
He will not resign the throne and usurps
My share of my own house.
Now I am prepared, given what is mine,
To withdraw and disband my army,
Reoccupy my home for the allotted span,
Yielding it once again for an equal period
To him, and not to bring my scaling-ladders
Against the proud towers of Thebes,
Nor raze them and this city to the ground
490   As I *will* do if justice is denied me –
As I will surely do. The gods are my witness
That, having in all things acted justly,
I most unjustly have my homeland stolen from me.
It is an offense against heaven.
That is my grievance, mother. You have heard it
As it is, without elaboration.
I hardly think the dullest mind
Could fail to recognise the justice of it.

CHORUS. I listen as one not born a Greek,
But feel his cause is soundly reasoned.

500 ETEOCLES. If we all thought alike, there'd be no argument.
Justice? Rights? Men do not know such things.
They give them names, they do not act by them.
Let me be frank, mother. I will hide nothing.
I want one thing,

And I would pluck the sun and stars out of the sky
Or rake the underworld, to see I had it.
That thing is power, the power to be a king –
Something too precious, mother, to barter
With a brother when it is mine, I hold it.
What sort of weakness would it be
To let the great thing slip and settle
For a smaller? And to *him*, who comes here   510
Threatening violence and trampling with armies
Over our country? I could not stoop to it.
It would be shaming Thebes itself to hand him
My throne because I winced
At the sight of Argive spears. The wrong
Is his, mother, trying to negotiate
By force. Words will win all the sword can.
If on some other terms he wishes to live here
He may. But I will not consent,
When I might be king, to be his subject.   520
Let him do his worst. Let fire and sword
Take their course. Harness the horses. Fill
The plain with chariots. He knows I will not yield.
And if this is wrong, then wrong is best done
For a throne. Save morality for issues less tremendous.
JOCASTA. O son, O Eteocles – I am old, I know it . . .
Don't despise me for that, not now, not altogether . . .
We who have experience can sometimes
Speak wiser than youth. Oh why, child,   530
Grasp so at greatness? Do not. Ambition
Is the very soul of wrong. It enters in
Where there is harmony and happiness
And tears them apart, this spirit that drives *you*.
Others have rights too. Respect them. It were better
Far to do so. How is friend ever bound
To friend, city to city or ally to ally
Except as equals? How but as equals
Can men share this world as nature intended?
To have or have not, to be greater or less –
Each is foe to the other. Set them up

71

540 And the days of hate dawn.
Do we not weigh, measure, number our lives
By due proportion, by allotted share?
Does not night's dark eye divide with day
An equal pacing of their yearly round
Without resentment that each gives place to other?
They serve their turn humbly, night and day – but you!
You cannot bear to halve your inheritance
With him who inherited with you. Where's justice then?
You value kingship too much, though what is kingship
But power enjoyed above justice? Oh, why
550 Do you think it so great? Do you wish that men
Look up to you? Vainglorious wish!
Is it wealth you desire with all its cares?
What's wealth? 'More', only that. Just a word.
If you understood better, you'd know that enough
Is sufficient. We do not own our possessions
On this earth. We simply hold in trust
What the gods have given. And when they want,
They'll require them of us again. Wealth
Is not lasting. It's only for a day.
Come, if I put before you a choice,
560 And ask if you would be king or saviour of your city,
Would you say 'king'? But if this man beats you
And Thebes goes under when Argos attacks,
You will see this city smashed apart,
You will see its women raped by Argive soldiers
And dragged off for slaves
And Thebes will have only curses left
For that power you pursue, and all your greatness.
And you, Polyneices –
What misthought favours has Adrastus done you?
570 You were mad to come here. Would you sack Thebes?
Think . . .
If you win, which God forbid, how before heaven
Will you fashion your thank-offering to Zeus?
With what words will you dedicate the sacrifice
Of your conquered country? How will your trophies

Be inscribed – 'Polyneices has burned Thebes
And to the gods offers these shields' – thus?
O my son, don't give that memory to Greece!
And yet if you fail, if his cause overruns you,
How will you go again to Argos, leaving here
Thousands of Argive dead? Will they not say
'Fatal the wedding you gave your daughter, Adrastus.   580
For one girl's marriage, see – we are destroyed!'
O child, both courses you pursue are fatal –
You lose Argos or lose Thebes. Let go, let go,
The two of you. Don't reach too far. Two madnesses
Colliding crushes us all . . .

CHORUS. O all you powers above, prevent such terrors,
And set these sons of Oedipus at one!

ETEOCLES. No, mother, words are no use any longer.
We've wasted our time
And your goodwill gains us nothing.
I've laid down the only terms we could agree on –   590
I remain king here. I rule in Thebes.
So leave off your wearisome admonitions,
Let me be.
As for you – I warn you
To get out before you are killed.

POLYNEICES. Before I am killed? Who would kill me?
Who bears such a charmed life that
He could draw sword on me
Before getting killed himself?

ETEOCLES. I do.

POLYNEICES. I thought you would think so. But creatures like
you
Who cling to power, cling to life.

ETEOCLES. You come mightily supported against one
You rate so lowly.

POLYNEICES. The better general is he who's best prepared.

ETEOCLES. You take advantage of the truce to be arrogant.   600
It is all that saves you from death.

POLYNEICES. It saves you too. This one last time,
I claim from you my right and my throne.

73

ETEOCLES. I know of no claim. I stand by what is mine.
POLYNEICES. By what is more than yours . . .
ETEOCLES. I have spoken. The city waits for you to leave.
POLYNEICES. O altars of my fathers . . .
ETEOCLES. Which you're prepared to plunder . . .
POLYNEICES. Hear me!
ETEOCLES. Why should they hear you when you march against
them?
POLYNEICES. O temples of the gods of shining steeds . . .
ETEOCLES. Who loathe your name!
POLYNEICES. He denies me the land of my birth . . .
ETEOCLES. You came to destroy it.
POLYNEICES. It is unjust, O heaven, unjust!
ETEOCLES. Call on Mycenae's gods, not ours.
POLYNEICES. You were born godless.
ETEOCLES. But not, I think, my country's enemy.
POLYNEICES. No? When you cheat me and drive me out of it?
610 ETEOCLES. And intend to kill you. You forgot that.
POLYNEICES. Oedipus, my father, do you hear the wrongs I
suffer?
ETEOCLES. He hears the wrongs you *do*.
POLYNEICES. And you, my mother . . .
ETEOCLES. Her name should scald your tongue.
POLYNEICES. O my city . . .
ETEOCLES. Go. Go to Argos. Call on her.
POLYNEICES. I am going. Never fear. Mother, I thank you . . .
ETEOCLES. Get out of this city!
POLYNEICES. Let me see my father.
ETEOCLES. Never.
POLYNEICES. My sisters . . .
ETEOCLES. You'll not set eyes on them again.
POLYNEICES. O my sisters . . .
ETEOCLES. You call on them? You're their worst enemy.
POLYNEICES. Mother, farewell.
JOCASTA. Son, I can only fare in sorrow.
POLYNEICES. I am son of yours no longer . . .
JOCASTA. Is there no end . . .?
620 POLYNEICES. For this man dishonours me.

ETEOCLES. You are my dishonour.

POLYNEICES. Where will your battle-station be?

ETEOCLES. Why?

POLYNEICES. I will take my stand against you there, to kill you.

ETEOCLES. Good! We are of one mind at last!

JOCASTA. Oh no, my children, what will you do?

POLYNEICES. You will see.

JOCASTA. The curse of Oedipus!

ETEOCLES. Ruin seize all our house!

POLYNEICES. The time comes, it comes soon, when my sword
   Will be urgent with death. But the land that nursed me
                                knows,

   The gods above know, how piteously I have suffered.
   They see, yes, they see me now shamefully used,
   Not like a son of Oedipus, like a slave, spurned,
   Thrust out, dishonoured. Thebes, whatever becomes of you,
   You know I am not to blame – it is this man!
   This is the guilty man! I came here unwilling   630
   And unwilling leave. Apollo of the Crossways, I leave you.
   I leave you, city I love, friends of my youth, statues
   Of the gods we fed with offerings. Perhaps I will never
   See you again. But my heart's hope is awake and eager –
   This man must be killed, and I shall rule in Thebes!

ETEOCLES. Out! Get out! How truly our father called you
                            'Polyneices' –
   The 'man of strife'. The gods must have warned him of you!

CHORAL ODE II.

   Once there was no city here
   till Cadmus came
   Cadmus of Tyre came searching
   from far Phoenicia searching.
   There will be a sign given the god had said –
   a heifer a wandering heifer   640
   unbroken knowing no master.
   Follow, and where it stops
   that is your place,
   where it kneels and salutes the earth

build there your house.
The plain is harvest-heavy there
sweet streams gush from a grateful soil
the waters of Dirce tumble through meadows
green with springing seed –
it is where the great god Bacchus was born
650   when Zeus's lightning flashed through his mother's side,
where with slow-twining tendrils
the ivy wove a bower of green shadow
over the growing child
for the maidens of Thebes to worship ever after
in song
when they call in the Bacchic dance his name
Evoe!

And so it happened,
and Cadmus came down to the stream called Dirce
for consecration.
And there was a dragon there to guard it
the War God's dragon
threatening death in the glittering eye
660   that scanned and scanned the forbidden waters . . .
A blow a great rock the head
crushed smashed –
with a hero's strength he killed it
Cadmus killed it . . .
Then there came in his mind's ear the voice
of the goddess Pallas Athene prompting –
'Pull the dragon's teeth from its jaw
and like seed
scatter them over the furrowed earth . . .'
670   He took them scattered them and there rose
out of the black earth a terror, it sent up a harvest
of spear-tips crests shields swords
a race of warriors full-armed growing out of the ground
sprouting over the fruitful plain
in anger.
And slaughter raced among them

raced blind among them iron-hearted
giving them back to the earth that bore them
drenching with their blood the soil that briefly
briefly had sent them into the sun and showed them
once to the winds of heaven . . .
Till half remained, till half remaining
laid their swords at the feet of Cadmus
and bound themselves to him to build this city.

Epaphos, hear us!
child of Io child of Zeus
hear us crying with foreign tongues!   680
Come down come down
to the land you loved,
the race that raised to you this city,
who are your sons.
And you Mother Earth, Demeter, Persephone
ruler of all, nurse of all
that springs from the soil
send the flame of your sacred torch
blazing through this land
and protect it and defend it,
o gods who can do
all things!

Scene Four
The Preparations for Battle

ETEOCLES. Bring Creon here, the Queen my mother's brother.   690
   Tell him I wish his counsel on matters
   Touching the state and on ourselves
   Before the raised spear calls us into battle –
   But no, he saves you the journey. I see him coming . . .
CREON. Sir, I have been everywhere, round all
   The city gates and every sentry, trying to find you.
ETEOCLES. And I, Creon, needed to see you. I met my brother   700
   And heard his terms of peace. They are quite worthless.
CREON. I was told so. Thebes is now, it seems, too small

For his ambition, with Adrastus behind him
And such an army. But that's as God wills.
My information is more pressing.

ETEOCLES. And what may that be?

CREON. We have an Argive prisoner . . .

ETEOCLES. Who can tell us what they're up to?

710 CREON. They're planning to encircle us, to throw
A ring of steel round the whole city.

ETEOCLES. Then we must attack. Now. Waste no time about it.

CREON. You are impetuous, sir. Where would we attack,
How would we attack?

ETEOCLES. Across the moat. We can get at them there.

CREON. But our forces are weak. Theirs are strong.

ETEOCLES. Come, Creon, I know them. Their courage is
Where their mouths are.

CREON. Sire, Argos is famed and feared throughout all Greece.

ETEOCLES. You are too timid. I'd fill the plain up with their
dead.

CREON. I hope so. Indeed. But such a task
Would not be . . . unlaborious.

720 ETEOCLES. I'll not keep my army cooped up in this city
Doing nothing.

CREON. But we do need to plan, to deliberate wisely.
It is our only hope of victory.

ETEOCLES. You want me to consider other ways?

CREON. All other ways. We dare not depend on one alone.

ETEOCLES. What about an ambush, attacking by night?

CREON. As long as our retreat's secured, if it should fail.

ETEOCLES. You can't count on certainty at night, but
Attack does give you the advantage.

CREON. And it's more terrible at night if things go wrong.

ETEOCLES. All right, then. Take them around supper-time
And rush them with infantry.

CREON. A surprise, a brief skirmish. We need to annihilate
them.

730 ETEOCLES. They couldn't retreat. The river Dirce's too deep.

CREON. None of this helps to safeguard ourselves.

ETEOCLES. What about a cavalry charge against the main camp?

CREON. It's impregnable. It has a ring of chariots round it.
ETEOCLES. Dear gods! What am I supposed to do then?
Just hand the city to them?
CREON. No . . . no, of course not. But no prudent policy
Was ever built on a string of extravagant ideas.
ETEOCLES. Suggest a more prudent policy than my 'ideas'.
CREON. They say – I have been told – that seven of their
number . . .
ETEOCLES. Seven? What can they do with seven?
CREON. . . . . That seven have been chosen to lead a force
Against each of our seven gates.
ETEOCLES. And what do we do? Wait for them, helplessly?   740
CREON. You choose seven also, one for each gate.
ETEOCLES. With men at their command? Or are they
To be champions, and fight solo?
CREON. With men at their command. Select the best.
ETEOCLES. They'll need the best. They'll have scaling attempts
Against the walls to deal with.
CREON. Also captains under them, so they can delegate
responsibility.
ETEOCLES. And am I to appoint them for their courage
Or because they're good at 'policy' and plans?
CREON. Both, sir. Neither can survive without the other.
ETEOCLES. All right, we'll do it. I'll go round our seven gates
As you suggest, and set a chosen man at each
With forces to match what the enemy sets against him.   750
I'll name them later – now would be wasting time
With Argives camping beneath our very walls.
But the one they set against me, God willing,
Will be my brother. I am the one must fight him,
Subdue him to my spear. *I* must kill the traitor
Who comes here expecting to sack *my* city.
Creon, before I go – should anything happen to me,
I ratify herewith the marriage of my sister   760
Antigone to your son Haemon. See to it.
And you are my mother's brother. Need I say –
Look after her, for your sake and for mine.
My father I can't commend. His blinding

He brought on himself and he must live with it,
While we . . . his curse could kill us yet.
That's one thing we've not done. Summon Teiresias.
He could tell us about that, he might have a prophecy
Or an oracle or something about it . . .
770 I'll send your boy Menoeceus to fetch him.
He'll come sweetly for you, Creon, he'll talk to you.
But I've mocked his magic and mumbo-jumbo
Too often to his face. He bears me a grudge.
One charge I lay on you, Creon – on you
And this city. If our side wins, the body
Of Polyneices is not to be buried in Thebes,
Ever. Make the penalty death if it's tried,
And whoever tries it, however trusted.
I leave this with you. Now call out my guards.
780 Bring out my arms and armour. We go into battle.
The fight before us is a fight for justice
And victory will be ours. Let us pray
For the safety of the city. O spirit of wisdom,
Of all grace, kindest of gods, fair counsellor,
Protect us and take us now into thy care.

CHORAL ODE III.
War – war and death
panic and blood and death . . .
Tie up your hair put away the flute
stifle the song in your throat
stop the dancing
all the sweet service of Dionysus.
War calls another tune and a different dance
without flutes.
There are Argive armies snuffing the air
790 for our blood,
there's a rattle of harness a clatter of hooves
and chariots thundering up past the bend in the river,
men are massing beneath the old stone walls
and they dance with shields, they sing to the sword
and they hate us.

Thebes has known nothing but trouble.   800
Up there among the secret glens on Cithaeron
up near the snow-line peer through the leaves
scatter the shy things in their thickets
and what will you find?
A child cradled a babe
with the scars of gold hooks on him –
Oedipus.
Who was never meant to live.
Why did he have to live?
Then another affliction –
the witch-bird swooping down from the high crags
the Sphinx screeching out of the sky
clinging with clawed hands and clawed feet
to the ramparts
snatching away our children
off into the untrodden blue.
Hell sent her against Thebes.   810
Why was she sent?

And now new strife new discord
because two brothers quarrel,
rampant like a poisonous weed
in the house of Oedipus
all through the city
from the fault of a birth a blinding
an incestuous bed . . .

Can you win through, city of the Dragon Men –
can you pluck honour out of your shame   820
find a new glory in your ancient grief?
You once knew a day when the Sons of Heaven
stood all around at Cadmus' wedding feast,
you knew a day when Dirce and Ismenus
watering the green plain at your feet
heard Amphion's lyre raise your walls to music.
Yes, Thebes had kings descended from Io
as I am descended.

830 Once Thebes stood high
and was honoured and was glorious
and war crowned her with triumph.

Scene Five
The Prophecy of Teiresias

TEIRESIAS. On, daughter, lead on. You are the eye
For my blind steps like a star is to sailors.
Forward. But keep to the level places
So I don't stumble. I don't feel very strong.
You have my writing-tablets? And the lots
840 I was casting at my seat of prophecy
To chart the oracles the birds were giving me?
Hold them safe. Where's Creon's son?
I hope it's not much further to the city
And your honoured parent, young Menoeceus?
My knees are folding under me. I've come so far
I can't go on much longer.
CREON. Hold up, Teiresias,
You've come to port now. You're among your friends.
Take his arm, Menoeceus. Old men and mule-carts –
Both alike! Won't move if there's no hand to help them.
TEIRESIAS. Creon? Oh, so we're here. Why the urgent
summons?
850 CREON. All in good time. I'm not forgetting it.
Get your breath back first. Throw off
The way's weariness and collect yourself.
TEIRESIAS. I'm worn out with work. Yes. Only yesterday
I was away helping Erechtheus' sons.
They had a war on too. Against Eumolpus.
I gave victory to them. See this gold crown I'm wearing?
They gave it to me from the spoils they took.
CREON. I take it as an omen in our favour.
You know how we stand, Teiresias. The waves engulf us.
860 The enemy are all around. Thebes is sore pressed.
Our king has himself gone down to the battlefield
To face them, and they are strong. But Eteocles

Charged me to find out from you
What our best course might be to save the city.
TEIRESIAS. Eteocles? If it's him, my lips are sealed.
I'll read no oracles for him. But if it's you,
If you seek enlightenment from me . . . I'll tell you.
It's diseased, Creon. This city has the plague.
It's had it ever since the gods were flouted
And Laius fathered a mate for his own wife
And Oedipus was brought into this world.
All that horror of blinding and blood –   870
It was heaven's warning to Greece.
Did they think they could cover it up?
Did his sons think, with time, they'd side-step the gods?
They hoped to, but they were wrong, the arrogant whelps.
They despised him, yet they wouldn't let him go.
They goaded his misery to fury, and he cursed them,
Out of his torment and shame, he cursed them.
What did I not do, what did I not tell them?
And for what? They hated me.
But death has crept up on them, Creon. It's close.   880
And they will kill each other.
And before they have finished – on both sides,
Dung-heaps of dead.
And there will be wailing and shrieking in the land,
And you, O Thebes, no more than a crumbling graveyard.
Hear me and be warned. Be rid of them,
All of them. None, no not one, of Oedipus' house
Must stay here – not as kings, not as meanest citizens.
They are doom-ridden. They can only wreak havoc.
And it spreads now. The evil spreads and
It will overpower you. True, there is
One resource left you, one hope only,   890
One way to escape. And yet . . .
To speak it would not be safe, even for me.
And for him who could heal all, who holds
The future of Thebes in his hand – it would be ruin.
I shall go now. Farewell. I am only one among many.
I'll endure what may be. What else can I do?

CREON. No, Teiresias, don't go.

TEIRESIAS. Take your hand off me.

CREON. Why do you desert us?

TEIRESIAS. Fortune deserts you, not I.

CREON. There's a way to escape, you said so. Tell it to us.

TEIRESIAS. You want me to? You won't want me to, soon

enough.

900 CREON. I want my city to survive.

TEIRESIAS. You are sure you wish to hear it?

CREON. How could I wish for anything else?

TEIRESIAS. Then I will read the future for you.
But first I must know one thing. Menoeceus
Brought me here. Where is he now?

CREON. At your side. Come closer, boy.

TEIRESIAS. No. Tell him to leave us, where
He cannot hear what I shall reveal.

CREON. He is my son, Teiresias. He will repeat
Nothing he should not.

TEIRESIAS. You insist that I speak in his presence?

910 CREON. I do. He is eager too to know what may save us.

TEIRESIAS. Hear then the way of prophecy,
What could be done to save Thebes.
You must see Menoeceus here
Slain for his country's sake. Your son . . .
Menoeceus . . . You demanded to be told.

CREON. What . . . did you say?

TEIRESIAS. What is ordained. What you have to do.

CREON. You are brief for such a tale of horror.

TEIRESIAS. It may be that for you. It is salvation for your

country.

CREON. I did not hear it. I was not listening.
Thebes can take care of itself.

920 TEIRESIAS. Is that Creon? I don't recognise him.

CREON. Peace be with you, but go now.

TEIRESIAS. This is a frightened man.

CREON. I can do without your divinations!

TEIRESIAS. Is truth destroyed because it distresses you?

CREON. O Teiresias, I clasp your knees, I touch your beard . . .

TEIRESIAS. Why kneel to me? The only other way is ruin.
Do you pray for that?
CREON. Only keep silent. Do not tell this to the city.
TEIRESIAS. That would be wrong. You cannot ask it of me.
Silence is no longer possible.
CREON. What will you do to me? Will you murder my son?
TEIRESIAS. Others must see to the doing, I only speak.
CREON. But why, Teiresias? Why me and the boy here?
What happened to bring this horror upon us?
TEIRESIAS. Yes, it is right to ask. You are right to challenge me.   930
There is a place where the earth asks for blood,
A deep place in the earth, still demanding a death,
Which only this boy can give. Long ago
A dragon dwelled there, guarding the springs of Dirce,
And it was sacred to the War God. Cadmus killed it,
And in all these years the god has not forgotten.
Give him a death for that death, and War becomes
Your ally. Make that earth rich again. It needs
Living blood for the blood of life it gave
When Cadmus sowed it with the dragon's teeth
And it sent up for him a harvest of armed men   940
To populate his city. One of that race
Must pay this death, and of the Dragon Men
Descended direct, of pure blood on both sides,
You only – you and your two sons – survive.
Haemon is exempt, he is not virgin.
Though his marriage is not solemnised, he is contracted.
But this boy is as yet pledged only to the city.
His sacrifice could save it.
Adrastus would turn home in ruin.   950
Night would close up Argive eyes.
Thebes would be made glorious.
There is your choice. Save which one you will,
The city or your son. You have all I can tell.
Take me home, daughter. What's the sense
In practising my visionary art? A man's future
Shows disaster, and you're hated for revealing it.
But if you pity him and lie,

You wrong your sacred calling. The gods
Should do their own interpreting to men.
They have no one to fear.

960 CHORUS. So silent, Creon?
Can you not form the words?
Too shattered for speech, are you?
Yes, I can feel for you.
CREON. What word can there be? No, it is clear
What my word is. I will not rush into ruin.
Offer the city my son's life? Never!
I love him. As any man loves his child.
Who hands his child to death? Who thinks
To slay mine and say that I do well?
It is I who am prepared to die. My life
Makes a fitter and riper sacrifice for Thebes.
970 Menoeceus, make ready, before they all hear of this.
Forget the old man and his mad mumblings.
You must escape, as fast as may be. Fly the country.
He'll go the round of the gates and guard-posts
Telling everyone. If we can forestall him,
You're safe. If not, we're both undone.
It will be your death.
MENOECEUS. Where shall I escape to?
A city somewhere? Or friends?
CREON. Wherever you're furthest from reach of here.
MENOECEUS. Tell me what to do, and I will do it.
CREON. Get beyond Delphi, first . . .
980 MENOECEUS. Yes?
CREON. And into Aetolia . . .
MENOECEUS. Where then?
CREON. Make your way to Thesprotia . . .
MENOECEUS. Where the sacred wood is . . .?
CREON. Where the sacred wood is at Dodona.
MENOECEUS. Will I be safe there?
CREON. You will be under the protection of Zeus there.
He will guide you.
MENOECEUS. How will I provide for myself?

CREON. I will see you have money. I will get you some.
MENOECEUS. It is good what you say, father. Hurry then.
    I must go first to your sister, Jocasta,
    And say goodbye to her. She was a mother to me
    When I was orphaned. Then I'll escape.
    But hurry now. You would not delay my going . . .   990

    I did that well. My words were false
    To take away his fear, and win my own way.
    He'd steal me out of here, cheating the city
    Of its only chance, branding me coward,
    Which might be pardonable in someone old
    But would be unforgivable in me.
    Turn traitor to Thebes? No. It gave me birth
    And I will save it. Count on that.
    I am going now to offer up my life,
    To die for my country. Men face death for that
    Who have no prophecies to prompt them.
    They stand unflinching in the ranks of battle
    Fighting for our city, and no fate forces them.   1000
    Shall I then betray my father, brother,
    Thebes itself, and fly like a coward?
    I would not dare such dishonour. Where
    Could I ever live and not be pointed at
    For what I'd done, for all my life?
    O Zeus among the stars, O murderous Ares,
    Who set Earth's harvest of the dragon's teeth
    To be this kingdom's rulers – I am coming.
    My stand will be upon the rampart's top
    High above that deep place in the earth   1010
    The prophet spoke of, which the dragon guarded.
    There I will kill myself and set my country free.
    It is spoken.
    The life I give this city is honourable
    And pure, it will purge her sickness.
    If men would only give, each in his power,
    Their good for the good of all, this world
    Might suffer less, go forward hoping.

CHORAL ODE IV.

> Out of an innocent sky came terror
> came terror
> with a slow flapping of wings,
> a thing that was born of darkness
> that came up out of the pit
> monstrous
> to drink Theban blood,
> bringing terror
> bringing horror –
> half woman
> but an animal a beast
> with wings
> circling slow-flapping wings
> and claws to tear flesh with.
>
> And one day she appeared suddenly
> the Sphinx
> out there beyond the river Dirce
> and started swooping on children
> and carrying them off . . .
> That cry that wild bird-scream
> that scream as she made her kill
> kill kill!
> And Thebes whimpered for fear.
>
> What murdering murderous god
> ordained such things
> allowed such horrors to happen?
> Mothers cried out and wept
> the young women cried out and wept
> homes rang with weeping
> cry cry!
> weep aloud aloud!
> cry one to another through the stricken city!
> Grief raging like a storm
> a tempest of lamentation
> as the winged she-devil

1020

1030

1040

snatched our children
and vanished with another
and another.

Then one day
came striding into Thebes
striding like a hero
with the voices of gods in his head
Oedipus –
fateful Oedipus.
Oh the joy then
the weeping with relief!
It was later the horror came back
when he lay with his mother.
But he was the bright champion
who beat the Sphinx
broke her power
untwisted her riddle.

Yet there had come into the city
something unclean   1050
blood
and a curse
passed on in curses
on his sons
and bitter hate
and strife.

Give thanks
give thanks now
for one who goes to his death
for Thebes' sake
to purify Thebes.
Creon is left to weep
but Thebes is set proud again
in triumph.
Pray for sons as noble   1060
pray that the long curse be lifted.

O Pallas look with favour on us –
you quickened Cadmus' courage
you sped the dragon-slaying rock.
And yet
we have known too long
there is some god
hates us.

Scene Six
The Battle for Thebes

MESSENGER. Ahoy there! Who's guarding the gate?
Open up, someone. Call out Jocasta. Ahoy there, open!
1070   Come out and hear me, famed wife of Oedipus – this
Is what you've been waiting for. Leave your wailing and

tears.

JOCASTA. What is it, friend? O friend, what news?
But no, it is something terrible. It's Eteocles.
Aren't you his shield-man? Shouldn't you be
Beside him now, in the battle? Oh, is my son dead?
MESSENGER. If that's your fear, forget it. He's alive.
JOCASTA. How is the city then? Do our defences hold?
MESSENGER. Unbreached as yet. Thebes keeps her honour safe.
1080 JOCASTA. But there was danger?
MESSENGER. Oh, it hung on a knife's edge. But we
Were the stronger. We Cadmaeans
With fight inside us can outmatch Mycenae.
JOCASTA. Tell me one thing – what do you know
Of Polyneices? His life is my care also.
MESSENGER. So far they both survive. Both. So far . . .
JOCASTA. Bless you for that. But how have the Argives
Been held back? Tell me, so I can go
To the blind old man in the house and give him glad news.
MESSENGER. There was a sign given to us – a death. It was
1090 Your brother's son, Menoeceus. We caught sight of him
Standing on the highest tower, saw him thrust his sword
To the black hilt through his own throat. He gave
His life for Thebes. That saved us, and the battle turned.

The king your son had posted seven companies,
Picked men and their captains, at the seven gates
To match the Argives, horse and infantry,
Each weighed against the other's with reserves
Ready to rush in wherever the defences weakened.
From the tower-tops we watched them, saw the white shields
Wheel past Teumessus, approach the moat and mass there.   1100
Then they charged, yelling their battle-cry,
And trumpets blared, and back from our own walls
Came the bray of answering trumpets, splitting the air.
First of our seven were the Neistian Gates to bear
The brunt, from a dense horde battering with shields
Brass-bound and spiked, and led by Parthenopaeus
Whose own was blazoned with the sign of Atalanta,
His huntress-mother, shooting the Aetolian Boar.
Against the Gate of Proetus came the warrior-priest,   1110
His chariot laden for the rites of sacrifice,
His shield mute of challenge, his ensign blank.
The Lord Hippomedon attacked the Ogygian Gate
Bearing a shield all eyes for Argus the All-Seeing –
Some opening as the constellations rise,
Some closing when they set, as close they did
When later, death eclipsed his own life's star.
Opposing the next gate – Tydeus: and across his shield   1120
A full-maned lion's pelt, with Prometheus figured
Upon it bearing fire to symbolise
The burning of Thebes. Against the Fountain Gate
Came your son Polyneices, with the fearful sign
On his shield (flexed by pivots against the hand-grip)
Of the mad and maddened flesh-eating Horses of Hades
Running wild. Next Capaneus, whose love of war
Rivals the War God's, led the attack against
The Electran Gate, and stamped out on his shield
With iron studs was one of the Earth Giants,   1130
Bearing a city entire upon his shoulders
Torn up from its foundation – he meant us to know
Our city was destined for no less a fate.
At the last and seventh gate stood Adrastus of Argos.

Now close by Argos lived the dreaded serpent
Of the hundred heads, the Hydra, and that was displayed
Upon his shield-arm as if from our Theban walls
It were snatching our Theban men in hungry jaws.
1140   These I saw while taking the password round –
Saw them all clearly as I see you.
The battle began with a rain of arrows and spears
And volleys of sling-shot, and stones crashing down
On all sides. At this stage we were winning,
When there's a shout – 'Sons of the Danaans' . . .
(it was Tydeus and your precious Polyneices)
'What are you waiting for? We'll be strafed to tatters
By this shooting. All together now,
Foot, horse and chariots – charge the gates!'
They heard and were heartened. There was a sudden rally
And bloodied heads began hitting the dust in hundreds –
1150   On our side too, you could see them by dozens
All along the battlements diving to their deaths
And the parched earth turning slippery with blood.
Then Parthenopaeus, Atalanta's son –
He was from Arcadia, not Argos itself –
Came on like a whirlwind up against the gates
Yelling for fire and axes to tear the town apart with.
But he was halted in mid-yell by that son
Of a sea-god, Periclymenus, tumbling a rock down on him
Big as a wagon – just tipped it over
1160   The lip of the parapet, and his gold head cracked open
Like a crushed nut coming apart. One second a face,
The next a purple pulp. *He*'ll not carry
A proud life back to his huntress mother in the mountains.
Well then, Eteocles could see that at this gate
All went well, so on he passed to the next,
With me close behind. And there was Tydeus
With a swarm of his shieldmen, keeping up
Such a barrage of those Aetolian javelins of theirs
Against the topmost tower-face, that men
Were deserting the outer battlements in panic.
Oh, but that son of yours – he could have been a huntsman

92

Whistling up his hounds! He rallied them round again
And packed them back to their posts. So that   1170
Stopped the rot there. And on we hurried to other gates.
Now Capaneus – how can I best describe Capaneus?
He was mad, raging mad. He was way up
One of the tallest scaling-ladders, clinging and climbing,
And how that man ranted! Not Zeus himself,
No, not God's own thunderbolts were going to stop him
Grinding our town to rubble. And all the while
Up he came, jabbering on, stones pelting down on him
Bunched beneath his shield, rung after rounded rung
Up that ladder. He's at the top, head level with the coping   1180
                                                            now
And coming over when – the lightning struck!
There was a deafening crash, the earth shook
And everyone ducked for dear life. And there –
Sailing out from the wall – wheee! like a shot from a sling
Went Capaneus cartwheeling, hair in the wind,
Blood showering down, spinning spread-eagled
Like old Ixion on his wheel.
He was dead when he hit the ground. Burnt out.
A shrivelled cinder.
Well, that convinced Adrastus Zeus wasn't on *his* side
And he smartly pulled his forces back beyond the ditch.
But to us the portent showed heaven was helping
And out we sallied again. Our horse and chariots   1190
Charged. With a solid phalanx of spears
Against their infantry, we smashed into their centre.
It was a massacre. Men cut down and dying,
Slumped across chariot-rails, wheels bucking,
Leaping, axle piled on axle, mounds of dead –
All heaped together in confusion.
So for today at least we've beaten them back,
Our defences have held. It's in the lap of the gods
If Thebes' good fortune lasts, but some god
Surely helped her to survive till now.
CHORUS. Gods looking fair on Thebes may look fair on me.   1200
Shall I not now hope for myself too?

JOCASTA. Heaven and fortune both are merciful.
I still have my sons. Our city has escaped.
Only my poor brother, who gave me to Oedipus,
Reaps a harvest of loss. He mourns a son
For whom Thebes must give thanks. Have you more to tell?
What does Eteocles intend?

MESSENGER. The rest can wait. So far all's well and you've been
lucky.

1210 JOCASTA. What do you mean 'so far'? No, it can't wait.

MESSENGER. What more do you want? Your sons have not been
killed.

JOCASTA. I need to know if I can trust what's coming.

MESSENGER. I must go. Let me go! I left the King unattended.

JOCASTA. There's something wrong. You're hiding something
from me.

MESSENGER. I brought you good news. Why should I now tell
you bad?

JOCASTA. Why should you not sprout wings and fly? Now tell
me.

MESSENGER. You should have let me leave after the good things.
Why add the rest? All right. Your sons intend -

1220 It's wild, it's wicked of them – to fight it out on their own.
No armies. Single combat. To both sides
They've said it now, and who can unsay it?
Eteocles began it.
He called to the Argive army from high on the ramparts
For silence to let him address them. 'Danaans' he cried,
'You who have come here, captains from the whole
Of Hellas, and you too, people of Thebes,
Why should you sacrifice your lives either
For Polyneices or for me? It is wrong.
I foreswear that sacrifice and will myself

1230 Do battle alone with my brother. If I kill him
I reign alone. If I lose, to him alone
I yield the kingship of Thebes. Abandon this fight,
Men of Argos, leave Thebes in peace, do not die here.
Enough already have died of Cadmus' line.'
He'd hardly finished before your son Polyneices

Had leapt to his feet to praise and support what he'd said.
The Argives all cheered their approval, so did we,
For it sounded just. And truce was called there and then,   1240
With both armies' generals meeting out in neutral
Ground between them to swear how solemnly
They'd honour it. Then began the arming
Of the two protagonists, they whose youth
Was acting out their father's ancient doom.
Each had their friends to help them. Limb by limb
They were lapped in bronze, strapped into glittering war-gear,
Thebans aiding the Theban, Argives his brother,
Till both stood forth shining, the hot blood flushing
Their cheeks, each with his own supporters clustering
Round to egg him on, with 'Now, Polyneices,
You can set up your trophy to Zeus, make Argos famed,'   1250
Or 'You are your city's champion, Eteocles,
Conquer and stay king.' And as they urged them on to battle,
Sheep were slain upon altars, and the priests
Began divining what the sacrificial flames
Portended – how many leaping tongues or clefts,
Whether they fizzle with damp (an evil sign)
Or throw up a halo of light (and that could mean
Either thing, a victory or a disaster).
Oh madame, your help is needed. Wise words or prayers,
Magic or spells, anything you can. Hold back your sons   1260
From so awful a struggle. The danger's great.
What grief more than this could you win today
Than both your sons dead . . .?

JOCASTA. Antigone! My daughter! Fetch me my daughter!
Oh, my innocent girl. This is where childhood
Ends. The gods are closing in.
Two marvels of men have told death they're coming,
And they are blood of your blood.
But you and I, daughter, are going to stop them,
You and I both. They must not kill each other.

ANTIGONE. Mother, what is it? Why are you out here?   1270
I heard a new terror in your voice.

JOCASTA. Your brothers' lives run out.

ANTIGONE. I don't understand.

JOCASTA. They are met for single combat.

ANTIGONE. What are you saying?

JOCASTA. Nothing of comfort. Come with me.

ANTIGONE. Where to?

JOCASTA. The battlefield.

ANTIGONE. Oh, mother, how can I? Must I leave this house,
Must I face those people? They frighten me.

JOCASTA. Come, girl, this is no time for maiden modesty.

ANTIGONE. What . . . am I . . . to do?

JOCASTA. Stop your brothers fighting.

ANTIGONE. I don't know how.

JOCASTA. Do what I do. We'll fall at their feet together.

ANTIGONE. Show me where we go. Let us not lose time.

1280 JOCASTA. Quick then, daughter, quick. Oh, I can live again
If we forestall them. If not, their death is mine.

CHORAL ODE V.
    Fear . . .
            fear . . .
                    shakes me.
  Over my skin crawls
  pity, pity for that tortured mother.
  Which of her sons will kill her son?
1290 O Zeus, O Earth . . .
  blood-brothers,
  brother's blood,
  which can I weep for?

  Two wolves howling for the kill,
  the rattle of two spears poised for the death-throw,
  and the slow sad stain in the dust.
1300 We can wait only to weep only to cry out,
  even we who are strangers.
  Death is so close.
  Death willed by the Furies.
  The last horror
  for day to reveal.

Hush now, hush. Leave off our tears
And whimpering. Creon is coming.
Poor Creon. The shadow has fallen upon him.

Scene Seven
The Death of the Brothers

CREON. Which am I to weep for first –   1310
  Myself or my city, both like lost souls
  Crossing to the dead shore.
  Look. Here is my son. Sacrificed for Thebes.
  His name will be for ever glorious, but to me
  A never-ending pain. He lay on the Dragon Rocks,
  And I took him in my arms, gathered him, cradled him.
  There is a cry goes up from all my house.
  I have grown old. I come to seek comfort of the old.
  Where is my sister, the Queen, Jocasta, to lay out
  My dead son? The dead must have their due
  From us who are old but still not dead.   1320
  The gods below must have their due.
CHORUS. Jocasta has gone, Creon. Antigone with her.
CREON. Gone? Gone where? And why have they gone?
CHORUS. She heard her sons were to fight it out –
  Who would be king – in single combat.
CREON. What are you telling me? I did not know,
  I did not know this too . . . I had my son . . .
CHORUS. And time has passed now since her leaving.
  The fight could be ended . . .   1330
CREON. Must I bear this also, the sign approaching
  That it is true? A man comes running
  With news. And fate in his eyes . . .
MESSENGER. Oh God, how am I to tell what I have to tell?
  I bring a burden of grief, nothing but grief.
CREON. We know grief already. What would you tell?
MESSENGER. Oh, Creon, your sister's sons are dead.
CREON. Do you hear that, house of Oedipus?   1340
  You too! Your sons too are dead!
CHORUS. Would the walls themselves not weep

Did they but know?

MESSENGER. And to that sorrow add sorrow.

CREON. Have you more?

MESSENGER. Your sister died with her sons.

CHORUS. Ahee!

1350   Wail, howl, beat the head in mourning!

CREON. Jocasta, O Jocasta, O my sister . . .
    That it should all end here and all the curse
    Come true. What happened to them?

MESSENGER. It had gone so well. You know how we beat back
    The attack on the towers. From the walls there, you could see it.

1360   But then the brothers, resplendent in full armour,
    Had come out together into the dead ground
    Between the armies, ready to fight it out alone.
    And Polyneices looked towards Argos
    And called on the Queen of Heaven . . .
    'Dread Hera, I am thine now,
    Thine since I wed the daughter of Adrastus
    And dwell in his land. Grant me
    To kill this brother. Grant that my hand
    Signal its victory, stained with my foe's blood.'
    It was so terrible a prayer, so awful the trap

1370   Which fate had caught them in, that many felt tears,
    And in that watching crowd, glances met
    As if in shame, and had to look away.
    But Eteocles was looking towards Thebes, his home,
    And he called on Athene of the golden shield –
    'Daughter of Zeus, guide thou my hand. Let victory
    Sit on my spear. Let this arm loose it at my brother's breast
    And kill him who came here to lay my country waste.'
    It was like a beacon-blaze to signal the fight.
    A trumpet blared and they sprang at each other

1380   As if they were wild boars whetting their savage tusks
    And slavering at the mouth. They jockeyed
    For position, spears poised and quivering, but each
    Kept crouched within the circle of his shield,
    Offering no target. But if one saw the other's eye

Peer round the rim, in went the spear then
With a quick stab, quick jab, to get past his guard.
But they were both too cunning, using the eye-squints
In their shields. So, for a time, spears could do nothing.
And we, watching, waited and sweated,
Fearful, the lot of us, more than the fighters
We sweated for. Suddenly Eteocles flicked his foot,   1390
Scuffing a stone aside, and his leg showed
Out beyond the edge of his shield.
Polyneices saw it and struck,
Aimed straight for the hostage offered to his spear
And sliced the blade of it clean through his calf.
Up went a roar of applause from the whole Argive army.
But in lunging he'd exposed his shoulder
And Eteocles, wounded though he was, saw that and caught
                                                                    him
A blow between the ribs that staggered him,
So that the Thebans cheered in their turn.
But the spearhead broke, and with his weapon useless,   1400
He fell back a step or two, caught up a jagged stone,
Hurled it, and snapped the other's spear-shaft
Clean in two. They were evenly matched again,
Both without spears. Instantly two hands
Snatched for their swords. They closed and locked
With a crash of shields that rocked the ground.
But Eteocles had a trick he'd learned in Thessaly
And now he used it. As they heaved and grappled
He suddenly gave way, throwing his weight
Back on the left foot, but keeping his eye   1410
Watchful for the hollow of the man's belly opposite,
Then lunged on the right foot, forward, shot
The blade through his navel and felt it jar in the spine.
Polyneices in an agony doubled up, chest
Over stomach, and choking in blood, collapsed.
And Eteocles, victorious, exultant,
Stuck his sword in the ground and bent
To strip him of his arms, conscious
Only of that, not of himself.

And that was his undoing. For Polyneices,
With still a gasp left in him, had even in his agony
1420   Clung to his sword as he fell, and with a last convulsion
Reached up and sank it in Eteocles' bowels.
They lie there, the two of them, close beside each other,
With dust in their teeth, and no certain victory.

CHORUS. Weep yet for Oedipus, the grief of Oedipus –
Oh dark, blind king, your curse was heard and heeded.

MESSENGER. Hear now the grief that followed.
For where her sons were fallen and were dying,
1430   Came their mother running in anxious haste,
She and her daughter, saw the wounds,
Saw their death upon them,
And cried out for her sons and her vain help.
She threw herself down, she fell by each in turn,
She wailed, she wept her wasted love,
And by her all the while, like one
Who shielded her, their sister crying
To those so dear, those who left helpless now
Mother and unwed maid.
And Eteocles battled for breath, but forced
One dying gasp. For he could hear his mother
And stretched out an ice-cold hand to touch her.
1440   But no voice came. His eyes spoke only,
And tears to tell her his love.
But his brother was breathing yet, and
Gazed on Antigone and on his aged mother –
'We are lost, my mother. I weep for you,
And you, my sister. And for my brother dead.
Yes, I loved him. We became enemies,
But I did love him. Oh mother, bury me –
And you, my sister – here in my own land.
1450   I lost our house, but they will not deny me
That much of my native soil? You will
Persuade them? Mother . . . close my eyes . . .'
And he laid her hand over them, 'Farewell . . .
The dark is closing round . . .'
So both sad lives together ended on a breath.

And when their mother saw it, saw that the whole disaster
Was wound up, all her pent suffering spilled over
In one last, fearful act. She snatched a sword up
From the dead and thrust it through her throat.
So she lies now with those she loved,
Her arms in a last embrace about them both.
Almost at once a fierce dispute broke out   1460
Between the armies, Thebes shouting that our king
Had won, they Polyneices. Captains railed
At one another – was it not Polyneices' spear
Struck first? No, how can dead men claim a victory?
And none had noticed Antigone steal away . . .
Then the Argives rushed to arms, but we –
And well for us that we had made provision –
Had never laid ours aside. We fell upon them
Before their defence was ready, struck hard
Without warning along the whole army's length.
There was none could stop us. Men pelting for their lives   1470
Poured out across the plain, and blood
Gathered into pools where dead men lay
With spears in their backs. And so we beat them.
The battle trophies are going up already
To Zeus the Victorious. They're stripping the killed
Of their shields, and spoils are being sent
Into the city. But some even now
Make their way here, bringing Antigone
And her dead for us to mourn.
The battle is over, but for Thebes
That is a joy with no joy in it.

Scene Eight
Oedipus

CHORUS. Now no longer the words only,   1480
  No longer the troubled tongue telling of it.
  Here comes grief itself into your midst
  For you to see –
  Three dead brought here before the house,

Three who took their way together
Into the trackless dark.

ANTIGONE. Tear off the veil now,
No shame, no modesty,
No hiding the hot blood, the hot tears,
No shrinking from this death . . .

Take me in the dance, Dionysus,
I give myself to you dancing.

1490   Strip this band from my hair,
Untie the knot of my robe,
I bring you the dead in the triumph of despair.
Ahee!

O my brother, your fate and Thebes' fate
Spelled out together in that name of yours –
The dread design accomplished,
The house of Oedipus destroyed.

Your fretful striving was no striving,
But death given for death
In desolation and terror,
Lifeblood for lifeblood . . .
Come my city, my home,
Who will sing the lament with me,

1500   And add their tears,
And add their tears?
What singer can I call to join me
Who bring three, blood of my blood,
Slaughtered mother and sons?

Do you laugh to see them, you Furies,
Are you satisfied at last
Who have hounded our house,
Worked ruin for all the line of Oedipus,
Ever since that hour he caught out the Sphinx
In her riddle and stopped
The song dead in her throat?

O my father –
Who of all Greece, who

1510   Of all the noblest princes of this world
Ever in their brief day suffered

What you have suffered
With all men's eyes upon you . . .!
And I too am left desolate
To sing ever my song alone.
Not the bird that sits in the oak tree
Or perches in the high branch of the olive
Can match my mourning note,
Nor aid my sorrow.
For my mother is gone from me
And lonely the life I am left,   1520
Lonely the tears, the tears . . .
See, I tear my hair,
I lay it on the dead, an offering –
Which first?
On the dear dry breasts of my mother
Which gave me suck,
Or the gaping death-wounds
Of my brothers?
Ahee!
Father, O my father, come out!   1530
You are weary, old now and weary,
Groping your way endlessly round and round
That blind cage you made for yourself,
Dragging the weight of your life
Through that sleepless fog.
But now you must leave it,
Old Oedipus,
You must bring your ravaged, blinded face
Out here,
Into the light.

OEDIPUS. What do you want with me, girl,
Here in the open? My staff! My feet cannot see!
What right have your tears to drag me   1540
From my bed in the dark? I am only
A grey ghost of a thing,
A shadowless dead thing,
I do not belong out here
In this waking world.

ANTIGONE. You have got to know what has happened,
    What *is* out here.
    Your sons are dead, Oedipus.
    And your wife is dead who loved you,
    And was your staff and cared for you,
1550   And cherished your blind age.
OEDIPUS. Oh spare me, spare me more suffering!
    Three gone together? How, child, how?
ANTIGONE. Your curse – no, father, no blame,
    No reproaches, I weep for it like you –
    But it fell on your sons and crushed them,
    A fire that consumed them, a sword
    That cut them to pieces.
OEDIPUS. Oh my children! Ahee . . .!
1560 ANTIGONE. Yes, cry for them! Oh, had you eyes now
    To see the bright sun galloping overhead
    And here below, the bodies of the slain!
OEDIPUS. Their fate, my sons . . . I understand.
    But what of my wife?
ANTIGONE. She went down to them, went down
    To plead with them, plead with them
    In front of them all, crying out
    And weeping and baring her mother's breasts.
1570   It was just past Electra's Gate she found them,
    Where the meadow is thick with flowers,
    Fighting to the death like caged lions
    Clawing at each other's wounds.
    But their lives had drained from them already.
    War had poured its libation to Death.
    And she took from the cold hand its bronze-hammered sword
    And turned it on herself, despairing.
    She died embracing them. Oh, father,
1580   All in one day whatever power
    Spells out our fate has heaped the woes
    Of our house in one black woe together.
CHORUS. A day that brings disaster on Oedipus
    And all his line. O, lighten humanity's load!

CREON. It is time to leave mourning. The dead
   Call for burial. Oedipus, listen
   To what I must tell you now. Eteocles,
   Your son, appointed me his heir
   Here in Thebes. It was to be his dowry
   For Antigone's marriage to my son, Haemon.
   I cannot, for the sake of Thebes, permit you
   To live here longer. Teiresias said it plainly –   1590
   While you remain, Thebes cannot be well.
   You must go. I do not say this
   For your hurt. I am not your enemy.
   I simply fear the curse that follows you
   And the harm it could yet do us.

OEDIPUS. O fate, have you not from my beginning
   Bred me wretched beyond all men,
   Singled me out for suffering? My mother
   Had not laboured yet to bring me to the light
   Before Apollo told how I, unborn,
   Should kill my father, and he, my begetter,   1600
   Knew me as his destined death, tried to destroy me,
   Tore me from my mother's breast and threw me
   To the mercy of wild beasts on the bleak
   Mountain side. But I was saved.
   Saved! O you place of desolation,
   Why were you not sunk fathoms deep
   In hell for not destroying me?
   You let me go, let me be rescued,
   Cared for at Polybus' court, lovingly
   Led towards the horror of
   My fate's fulfilment. I killed my father,
   Bedded with my mother, got on her sons
   Who were my brothers, and whom I now   1610
   Have killed, passing to them
   The curse that Laius laid on me.
   What does heaven want of me?
   I was not born mad! Never could I
   Have done such things of my own nature,
   Against my eyes, against my sons,

If the whole cruel, senseless cycle
Had not been god-contrived against me!
Ah well, it's done. What do I do now
With this wasted shell? Who is to guide
The blind old man? She who's dead?
Were she alive she would, I know.
Or my fine sons? I do not have any.
Am I young enough still to earn my own bread?
1620   How? Creon, why slay me utterly?
For you do slay me if you cast me out.
But I'll not beg from you. I'll not
Go down on my knees to you. Wronged
I may be. I'll not demean my birth.

CREON. No, you must not kneel to me.
But I, too, cannot let you stay among us.
As to these two dead brothers, one
Must be taken now into the palace. The other,
Polyneices, for siding with our enemies
Against the safety of the state, is to be thrown out
1630   Beyond the city's boundaries and left
Unburied. This proclamation to Thebes –
'Any attempt to honour this corpse,
Lay wreaths on it or cover it with earth,
Will be punished with death. It is to be left
Unattended, unwept, for kites and vultures.'
Come, Antigone. We understand
Your distress, your triple loss.
Compose yourself now. Come indoors. The city
Grieves with you, but tomorrow you'll make Thebes
Rejoice again when Haemon and you are married.

ANTIGONE. Oh, father, this makes your wretchedness perfect.
1640   I could pity you even more than the dead,
Griefs crowd upon you unalloyed.
Creon, if you are to be the new authority
In Thebes, how can you wrong him so
And reject him so and make these barbarous
Decrees against the defenceless dead?

CREON. That decision was Eteocles', not mine.

ANTIGONE. It is still senseless, and you a fool to follow it.

CREON. I am executing what the King enjoined
Upon me. That is right and proper.

ANTIGONE. It's wicked. He decreed it out of malice and hate.

CREON. Throwing that one to the dogs is natural justice.   1650

ANTIGONE. It's not. It's revenge. And it's against the law.

CREON. Polyneices was a traitor to Thebes.

ANTIGONE. For that he has already forfeited his life.

CREON. And right to burial.

ANTIGONE. Why? He claimed the share of his own country
Which was due him. Where was the sin in that?

CREON. Antigone, he will not be granted burial.

ANTIGONE. Then I will bury him, whatever the state says.

CREON. You will bury yourself beside him.

ANTIGONE. Why not? We loved each other. That would be
                                     beautiful
And right, to lie together.

CREON. Restrain her, someone. Take her indoors.   1660

ANTIGONE. Take your hands off! I'll not let go of him.

CREON. This is sacrilege, girl. It's not for you to decide.

ANTIGONE. 'Thou shalt not outrage the dead.' Who decides
                                          that?

CREON. No one is to cover that body.

ANTIGONE. For his mother's sake, Creon, for Jocasta's sake . . .

CREON. You are wasting your time.

ANTIGONE. Let me wash him, let me only . . .

CREON. It has been expressly forbidden . . .

ANTIGONE. Bind up those hideous wounds . . .

CREON. To tend his body in any way.   1670

ANTIGONE. Beloved, at least on your dear lips, one kiss.

CREON. You desecrate your marriage!

ANTIGONE. Do you think I would live to wed your son?

CREON. You must. What else can you do? Where else can you
                                          go?

ANTIGONE. If you force me to it, I'll kill him.

CREON. You hear that, Oedipus? She'll say anything.
She abuses us all.

ANTIGONE. I swear it. By this sword of my brother's, I swear it.

107

CREON. Why, girl, is such a marriage
    So impossible for you?

ANTIGONE. I am going with my father. I will share
    His exile and his misery.

1680 CREON. That is generous in you. It is noble.
    But I cannot think it wise.

ANTIGONE. I will stay with him till death, and die with him.

CREON. Go, then. Go. Let my son be safe from you.
    Go with your father. Leave us. Leave Thebes.

OEDIPUS. He may not praise your spirit, child.
    I do. And your love.

ANTIGONE. How could I marry and see you go into exile alone?

OEDIPUS. Stay and be happy. I can bear my ills.

ANTIGONE. You are blind. Who would take care of you?

OEDIPUS. I'll go as fate guides me. Where I fall, I fall.

ANTIGONE. Ah, where is Oedipus now? And the famous riddle?

OEDIPUS. Gone. One day for glory, one to be destroyed.

1690 ANTIGONE. I must share in that.

OEDIPUS. You would share the shame.

ANTIGONE. Not shame, father. Honour.

OEDIPUS. Take my hand. Now guide me
    To where I can touch your mother.

ANTIGONE. Here. This is she.

OEDIPUS. O my unhappy wife . . . Mother, my mother . . .

ANTIGONE. All sorrows met in her.

OEDIPUS. Where do my sons lie?

ANTIGONE. Here. Side by side.

OEDIPUS. Lay my unseeing hand upon their faces.

1700 ANTIGONE. Now you are touching them.

OEDIPUS. O dear dead sons, as pitiable as your father . . .

ANTIGONE. O Polyneices, doubly dear to me . . .

OEDIPUS. It works to its end now. The last
    Of all that was foretold.

ANTIGONE. More yet was foretold?

OEDIPUS. I shall die in exile. On Athenian soil.

ANTIGONE. Attica will take you in? Where?

OEDIPUS. It is a hallowed place. Where the Holy Horseman
                                    dwells.

Called Colonus. Come, girl, you have chosen
To share the lot of your blind father.
Guide me on my way.

ANTIGONE. Give me your hand. I help you   1710
As the wind helps on the ship.

OEDIPUS. So, I set out. You and I together, child.
Now your trial begins.

ANTIGONE. My trial. Yes. Mine is the hardest trial
Of all the daughters of Thebes.

OEDIPUS. Where do we go? Reach me my staff.

ANTIGONE. This way, this way, with me.   1720
Like this, like this, your feet.
Your strength is like a dream.

OEDIPUS. Look at me, you who disown me!
An old man shamefully, pitifully hounded
From my home. O God, what I am made to suffer!

ANTIGONE. You suffer? You suffer? O, father, others
Have suffered too, because of a blindness before
You blinded yourself.

OEDIPUS. My name was sung to heaven. Was it blindness
To have seen into the Sphinx's riddle   1730
And guessed it and saved Thebes?

ANTIGONE. That is dead, father, it is forgotten.
It is no longer a glory.
Don't pride yourself now on what is past.
Always for you there has been waiting
This last anguish,
To wander the wilderness and, somewhere,
To die far from home.
But I leave a home where friends
Grew with me from girlhood,
And I weep tears of longing for them.
I go from my land a fugitive
From all my sex. That is my wilderness.

OEDIPUS. And a true heart is your fate.   1740

ANTIGONE. It may earn me a remembrance
As sad as my father's.
My fate is bound also to yours, my brother,

So wronged in death, abandoned and unburied.
I may die for it, father, but secretly tonight
I'll bury him. I must.

OEDIPUS. Go back to your friends.

ANTIGONE. They have shared my grief enough.

OEDIPUS. At the altars of the gods . . .

1750 ANTIGONE. I have wearied them with prayers.

OEDIPUS. Seek refuge at least in Dionysus. His holy place
Is in the hills, unknown to all but those
Who worship him.

ANTIGONE. Yes, there was a time I knew him.
I wore the fawnskin too with other Theban maids,
I danced the hills in Semele's sacred throng.
Not now. What can I offer him now?
I no longer have that homage in my heart.

OEDIPUS. Mark me, you Thebans! I am Oedipus –
Oedipus who read the famous riddle,
Who was the greatest among you.
Oedipus, who was the only one

1760 Could break the Sphinx's murderous hold on you
And did it alone! Look at me now!
Disowned, dishonoured. Fit only to be pitied.
And yet . . . pity's no use. Grieving's no use.
The gods decree and we are mortal.
There's no appeal.
We must bear it.

CHORUS. O sacred crown of life –
To win through!
Reward me and
Stay with me
To the end.

THE BACCHAE

Translated by J. Michael Walton

Characters

DIONYSUS
TEIRESIAS
CADMUS
PENTHEUS
SERVANT
FIRST MESSENGER
SECOND MESSENGER
AGAVE
ATTENDANTS
CHORUS OF ASIAN BACCHAE

This translation of *The Bacchae* was first performed in the
Studio Theatre of the Gulbenkian Centre at the University of
Hull on 23 November 1983 with the following cast:

DIONYSUS	Nicholas L. Phillips
TEIRESIAS	Peter Olowale Ojo
CADMUS	Jonathan Cowap
PENTHEUS	Simon Hudson
SERVANT	Laurence Abbott
FIRST MESSENGER	Chris Gilbertson
SECOND MESSENGER	Jonathan Styler
AGAVE	Meg McDonald
SOLDIERS	Neil Philby, Peter Byworth
CHORUS LEADER	Frankie Mullen
CHORUS	Caroline Allen, Caroline Evans, Michelle Hesketh, Louise Heywood. Kerrie Hunt, Ganiat Kasumu, Sally Lindsay, Alison Mayer, Ceris Morris, Julie Morris, Jackie Smart
Set designed by	Jane Blackburn
Costumes designed by	Ruth Stuckey
Masks designed by	John Harris
Choreographers	Nicholas L. Phillips and Meg McDonald
Assistant Director	Richard M. Shaw
Directed by	J. Michael Walton

Before the palace of Thebes. Enter DIONYSUS.

DIONYSUS. Here am I, Dionysus. Son of Zeus and Semele,
Cadmus' daughter, I have returned to this land of Thebes
where I was born from the lightning bolt. Now I stand by the
springs of Dirce and the waters of Ismenus, a god . . .
disguised as a man. By the palace I see my mother's memorial
smouldering with the deathless fire of Zeus, my mother who
proved only too mortal in the face of Hera's unrelenting spite.
Cadmus, my grandfather, I applaud, who had this tomb   10
erected on hallowed ground, but it was I who wreathed it
with this profusion of vine-leaves. I have left behind the gold-
rich lands of Lydia and Phrygia, deserted the sun-parched
shore of Priam, the Bactrian fortress and the cruel land of the
Mede. Through Arabia I came, prosperous Arabia, and
through all of Asia where Greek and foreigner mix in the lofty
cities by the shore. Now I have come to Greece, this city first. 20
The dances and ceremonies invented there to celebrate my
godhead, I now bring here. Here, Thebes, I have first
aroused to women's cries. These women of Thebes I first
dressed in fawnskin, placed the thyrsus in their hands, the
ivy-covered shaft. Why these? Because these sisters of my
mother, these aunts of mine, denied that I was born of Zeus.
The last who should have done so they defamed my mother
Semele, proclaiming my god-like birth a trick of Cadmus to   30
save a harlot-daughter's face. That was why, they said, Zeus
incinerated my mother, for her presumption. I have driven
them mad. Homes abandoned they all roam the mountains,
out of their senses, deranged: every last woman in Thebes, up
there amongst the rocks and the trees, witless and homeless,
Cadmus' daughters among them. Thebes will have to learn to   40
appreciate me and my rituals. My mother will receive her
recognition when all recognise me as divine. Cadmus has
grown old and bequeathed his throne to his grandson
Pentheus. This Pentheus wages holy war on me, offers no
libations, ignores me in his prayers. I am going to have to

115

50 show this Pentheus, show all of Thebes, what kind of a god I
am. And when I have succeeded, I shall move on. But if
Thebes takes it in mind to resist and drive my Bacchants
from the mountains by force, then I must be their general.
Which is why you see me now in human form.
Come now my women, come now my dears.
This is not Tmolus, Lydia you have left.
Come now my acolytes, my fawnskin fawners,
Drawn from far places, eager to serve me.
Rattle your castanets, clatter your drums,
Cymbals and tambours of Rhea, the great Mother.

60 Clash them and strike them. Batter the palace,
Din down on Pentheus for the city to see:
While I to the mountains depart by myself,
There to accompany the mad Maenad dances.

Exit DIONYSUS. Enter CHORUS.

CHORUS. Far from Asia, land of Asia,
Far from Tmolus, sacred Tmolus,
I have come and I cry,
I have come and I praise,
I laud the name of Bromius,
Dionysus.
I praise his name, I laud his name,
My task though a sweet one.
The burden is sweet as we praise his holy name.
Bacchios. Dionysus.

Where? What? Who can resist us?
Who on the road? Who in the doorway?
70 Beware. Let him beware.
Let him stand aside, say nothing, stay dumb.
One name we cry. Let none say another.
Dionysus.

Happy. Happy is the one. Blessed is the one
Who comes to know the mysteries,
The mysteries of the gods,
Who hallows life, who yields.

Who yields, lets the soul dance.
Pure is our dance in the mountains,
Purified the dancer in the name of Dionysus.
Sacred are the rites, secret rites for Cybele, the Mother.
Break through, yield. Break through, yield.   80
Break through with thyrsus aloft.
Serve him, serve Dionysus.
Come Bacchants, come.
Dionysus is your god, god son of god.
Escort him home, home from Phrygia,
Home to Greece, the broad streets of Greece.
Bring him home, your Dionysus.

Dionysus god. Mother labours.
Lightning flashes. Zeus destroys, but Zeus preserves.   90
Mother dies, but Zeus preserves.
Preserved from the fire, concealed in his thigh,
Fastened there with golden pin,
All too quick for jealous Hera's eye.
In due time, as Fate decrees,
He is born, but what a child,   100
What a child from Zeus's thigh.
A savage child with horns and serpents in his hair.
His Maenads wear them still,
The child, Dionysus.

Thebes, city of Semele, Semele's nurse,
Crown her with ivy, crown her with fir,
Crown her with evergreen, berry and flower.
Brandish the thyrsus, twine wool through the fawn.   110
Then free her to dance in the name of our god.
Free from the shuttle, free from the loom,
She waits for her leader, possessed by the god,
Dionysus.
And Crete with its deep holy birthplace of Zeus,   120
Crete where the Corybants first beat the drum,
Drummed and mixed drumming with Phrygian flute,
The sweet thunder from which they offered to Rhea,

117

A gift which she used as the true Bacchic note.
130 From her it was raped by the Satyrs' mad band,
Who created a dance for the god they adore,
Dionysus.

Sweet, sweet it is to run through the hills.
Sweet to wear the fawnskin.
Sweet to fall enraptured.
Sweet is the hunt, sweet the goat,
140 Sweet the taste, sweet the raw blood.
To run through the hills, through Phrygia, sweet,
To follow through Lydia the lead of our god,
Dionysus.
The earth flows with milk, the earth flows with wine,
With honey it flows.
The smoke is like incense from brandished brand.
Run, shout, scream and cry.
150 Dance and fly, hair streaming behind.
On Bacchae, on Bacchae.
Far from Tmolus, golden Tmolus,
Praise him, praise him, praise his godhead.
160 Sacred song and sacred dance,
Mountain high and mountain wide,
Deepest drum and shrillest pipe,
Celebrate his bolting flight.
Dionysus.

Enter TEIRESIAS.

170 TEIRESIAS. Gatekeeper. Are you there? Call Cadmus, son of
Agenor who left Sidonia to fortify this place. What's keeping
you? Tell him Teiresias wants him. He knows why I'm here.
We made a bargain, one old man to his elder, to dress up in
the fawnskin, thyrsus in hand and wreaths about our brows.

Enter CADMUS.

180 CADMUS. I thought it must be you, old friend. I heard your
voice indoors. Sounds words from a sound man. Here I am,
fit and ready, all dressed up as the god requires. After all he
is my daughter's boy, Dionysus, revealed to man as a god,
and we must do our best by him. Where should we go and

118

dance, do you think, shaking a leg, and an aged head if it comes to that? You had better lead, Teiresias. We are neither of us as young as we were, but you are the clever one. I feel I could dance day and night, non-stop, beating the ground with my thyrsus with never a thought of how old I am.

TEIRESIAS. I share your enthusiasm. I feel young and I shall   190
                              dance.

CADMUS. Excellent. Let's fetch my chariot to take us to the mountains.

TEIRESIAS. No chariot. We would dishonour the god.

CADMUS. No chariot. I'll help you along then, one old man with another.

TEIRESIAS. We shall not weary. The god will be leading us.

CADMUS. Will we be the only men dancing for Bacchios?

TEIRESIAS. We are the only ones in our right minds. Not the rest.

CADMUS. We may as well get moving. Take my hand.

TEIRESIAS. Where are you? There. Now do not let go.

CADMUS. I am only a man. I cannot make light of a god.

TEIRESIAS. It is not for us to reason about the gods. We hold   200
what our fathers held, and their fathers before them, from time immemorial. They did not waste time rationalising and philosophising. Suppose someone says I look a fool at my age going off to dance with ivy in my hair. It is no shame to me. The god has decreed we should dance, young and old, and dance I shall. No half measures for this god, and no one is exempt.

CADMUS. Being blind you will not have seen him, Teiresias, so I   210
had better warn you. Pentheus is coming, my grandson to whom I resigned my power. He looks in a hurry. I think he may be cross. Bad news perhaps.
Enter PENTHEUS attended.

PENTHEUS. I only have to leave town, go away for a few days, and what happens? What's this I hear about strange goings-on, women leaving home to roam around the mountains, prancing through the trees in honour of this novelty-god Dionysus, who ever he may be? And, of course, in the midst   220
of all this revelry, drink. Then off they creep to bed down

with some man in a quiet corner. Dionysus? It is the goddess
of lust they are celebrating. I've caught some of them,
chained them up. There they stay in the public prison. As for
the rest, Ino is among them, Actaeon's mother Autonoe, and
230 even Agave who bore me to my father Echion. I will hunt
them down, and when I have them safe under lock and key,
I'll put a stop to this Bacchic nonsense. I hear too that some
foreigner has turned up, some comic-singer from Lydia, all
golden hair and perfume, flushed with drink and oh so
beautiful. It is he who debauches them night and day. When
240 I get my hands on him, I'll stop him swinging his twig. I'll
part his head from his neck. He is the one claims Dionysus is
a god, who was sewn in Zeus' thigh, when we know perfectly
well that the mother was blasted together with the child for
claiming Zeus as her lover. The effrontery of it. I don't care
who he is, hanging's too good for him.

    Oh, here's another marvel, Teiresias the prophet, all dolled-
250 up in a fawnskin. And my grandfather too. How ridiculous he
looks with that stick. Dear old man, I hate to see you so
unbalanced. Take off the ivy. Please. Give me the thyrsus.
Grandfather, please. This is your fault, Teiresias. It suits you
to introduce some new god, so you can pocket a commission.
If your senility did not protect you, I would lock you up with
260 the women for introducing these foul practices. It's always the
same. The moment you allow drink at a women's festival,
corruption takes over.

CHORUS. Profanity. Profanity. Strange man, have you no
  respect? Respect for Cadmus, sower of the earth-born,
  dragon-spawn. As Echion's son, do you scorn your house?

TEIRESIAS. A wise man with a good cause finds eloquence easy.
  You talk well enough, but there's no sense in your words.
270 Bold you may be, and capable too, but, without sense, a man
like you is a public liability. He is new perhaps, this god
whom you mock . . . but I cannot begin to tell you how great
his influence will be one day throughout Greece. You are a
young man. Listen to what I say. There are two main
principles in human experience, just two. The first is
Demeter, Mother Earth, or whatever you care to call her. She

120

nurtures man by the gift of solid food. Then there is Semele's
son who discovered wine, a liquid to match her mortal gift
with his, a gift to soothe the troubled mind and bring man
restful sleep, the best of all remedies. We pour libations so   280
that he, a god, may benefit mankind. Oh, you make fun, do
you, of that story about Zeus's thigh, and the baby sewn up
in it? Let me tell you the truth about that. It is a beautiful
story. When Zeus rescued Dionysus from the ashes, after the
lightning-bolt, he carried the baby off to Olympus. Hera
wanted to throw the god-like child out of heaven. Zeus, with
all a god's cunning, concocted this plan. Out of the ethereal   290
layer which surrounds the earth, he constructed a surrogate, a
phantom child which he gave to Hera, thus protecting the real
Dionysus from his wife's anger. But in time men confused
'ethereal layer' with 'laid in the thigh', a simple error of
transmission. So myths are made. Another thing you should
consider is that Dionysus is a god of prophecy. Bacchants,
like madmen, have method. When the man is entered by the
god, he can foretell the future. Or you could find Dionysus in   300
the province of Ares, god of war. Have you never heard of an
army, drawn up under arms, stricken with panic before it can
lift a spear? That is the 'madness' of Dionysus.

It is Dionysus you can see hurtling over the rocks at
Delphi, hair streaming, wand shaking, his power already great
in Greece. Pentheus, listen. Do not be so proud as to think   310
that brute force is the only source of potency in man. It is a
diseased mind that sees power only in strength. Accept this
god in your domain, reverence him, crown him, worship him,
in his special way.

As for the women, Dionysus does not require chastity, but
a temperate mind controls any circumstance. Take note of
that. The Bacchic rites alone never lead to corruption. You
know yourself what a joy it is to stand at your gates before a
cheering multitude. No harm in that. Allow him, then, his   320
due, the respect which pleases him. Cadmus and I, decked
out in our finery, we will dance for him. An aged pair but,
laugh as you may, we will dance. Nothing you can say will
make us oppose a god. It is you, alas, who have lost your

sanity, sick beyond drugs to cure.

CHORUS. Wise words, old man. Apollo could not grudge your reverence for Dionysus, a mighty god.

330 CADMUS. My boy, I tell you, Teiresias offers good advice. Go along with us. Abide by our custom. Come down to earth, think again. There is this too. Even if this god is really not a god, as you believe, you could at least say that he is. It's a worthy white lie. Semele gave birth to a god, and our family gets the credit. You saw what happened to your cousin, Actaeon, torn to pieces by the man-eating hounds he had reared. And you know why he suffered. All for claiming he

340 was better than Artemis at hunting. May you never suffer like that. Come, let me crown you with ivy. Join us in honouring the god.

PENTHEUS. Leave me alone. Go on. Dance about, if you must. I want none of this foolishness. But the man who taught you this folly, he shall get what he deserves. Go immediately to his seat of prophecy, and flatten it. Use crowbars if you have

350 to. Leave nothing standing. Throw all his trumpery to the winds. Perhaps then he'll take me seriously. The rest of you, search the city. I want him found, this freak who infects our women, corrupting our beds. And when you catch him, tie him up and bring him here. We'll see how he revels in being stoned to death.

Exit PENTHEUS.

TEIRESIAS. Oh, you fool, you do not realise what you are saying. Witless before, you are now stark mad. Cadmus, we must go,

360 do what we can for the man, whatever his savagery: do what we can for our city, god preserve it. Pick up your staff and follow me. Help prop me up, and I'll support you. It would be dreadful for a pair of old men to fall over. Still we must go. Son of Zeus, Dionysus must be served. Pentheus' name means grief. That is not a prophecy, Cadmus. It is a fact. A foolish man. Foolish words. May he never bring grief upon your house.

Exeunt TEIRESIAS and CADMUS.

370 CHORUS. Reverence, queen of the gods,
Flying, gold-winged over Man.

Reverence, do you realise
Did you hear what Pentheus said?
Do you hear how he slights,
How he sneers at the name Dionysus?
Dionysus is Semele's son, blessed and crowned,
Lord of the dance and lord of laughter, 380
Redeemer from care at the feast of the vine,
And when the wine's drunk and the festival over,
He delivers the ivy-clad Bacchants to sleep.

What is the result of an unbridled tongue,
What is the end of lawless misjudgement?
The outcome disaster, only disaster.
A life lived in quiet, right-minded and calm,
Preserves the house and keeps it from harm. 390
The gods, far-off, still gaze upon men.
Overstepping the mark is simply fool's wisdom,
Gaining him nothing who chases too far.
This way lies madness, attempting the summit, 400
Ill-judged and ill-starred, crashing to earth.

Let me come, let me come to Aphrodite's isle,
To fairest Cyprus where love's charms are fashioned.
There hundred-tongued the rivers give richness
To land untouched by rain.
Or let me come to Pieria,
Lovely Pieria where the Muses live, 410
To the slopes of Olympus, the holy.
Bromius, Dionysus, lead me there, dancing god.
There to the home of Desire and the Graces.
Lead me where dancing to Bacchios is welcome.

Our lord, son of Zeus, delights in the feast.
One goddess I name who pleases him more.
Giver of comfort, giver of joy,
Allowing young men to relish their youth.
The goddess he loves is the goddess of Peace. 420
To rich and to poor he brings gifts of enchantment,
Gifts he bestows through the virtue of wine.

But the man who declines, by day or by night,
To live life as pleasure, he loaths.
430 Wisdom is keeping apart from the rational.
Grant me instead what the simple believe.
Enter SERVANT and DIONYSUS.
SERVANT. Pentheus, Lord Pentheus.
Enter PENTHEUS.
We've caught the prey you sent us after. Here he is, tame
enough. He made no attempt to escape, never turned a hair.
He didn't even pale, but stood there with a smile on his face
and told us to bring him here. He held out his hands. It made
440 my job easier, but I felt a bit ashamed and I told him so. 'It's
not up to me, friend,' I said, 'Pentheus sent me.' And then
there are those Bacchants you had locked up in the public
gaol. They've gone. They got free, and now they're leaping
about in the fields calling on their Bromius. The chains fell off
them. The doors unbolted themselves without a hand being
laid on them. This man . . . I tell you, there are a lot of funny
things going on in Thebes, and he's the cause. What you
450 decide to do about it, of course, that's up to you.
PENTHEUS. You're losing your wits, the whole pack of you.
Now I've got my hands on him, he'll not get away in a hurry.
So, my friend. You are not so bad-looking, I see, not as far as
women are concerned, which is why you came to Thebes, no
doubt. Such long hair. Not a wrestler, I think. All down your
cheeks. Very luscious. You do have pale skin. Not much in
the sun, are you, under-cover mostly, hunting Aphrodite?
Right then. We will start with where you come from.
460 DIONYSUS. That's easy enough, though nothing to boast of.
Have you ever heard of Tmolus of the flowers?
PENTHEUS. I've heard of it, the area round Sardis.
DIONYSUS. That is where I come from. I am a Lydian.
PENTHEUS. And these rites you bring to Greece, where do they
come from?
DIONYSUS. Dionysus initiated me, the son of Zeus.
PENTHEUS. You have your own Zeus, do you, for spawning new
gods?
DIONYSUS. There is only one Zeus, Semele's husband.

PENTHEUS. And were you awake when this Dionysus forced himself upon you, or was it in a dream?

DIONYSUS. I confronted him, face to face. He looked at me and gave me his mysteries. 470

PENTHEUS. Ah yes, mysteries. What sort of mysteries would they be?

DIONYSUS. They are secret except to initiates.

PENTHEUS. Then what are the benefits for his devotees?

DIONYSUS. Considerable, but you may not be told them.

PENTHEUS. You are trying to intrigue me.

DIONYSUS. These mysteries are not for the unbeliever.

PENTHEUS. You say you have had a good look at this god. What is he like?

DIONYSUS. Whatever he wishes. I cannot dictate his appearance.

PENTHEUS. That's no kind of answer.

DIONYSUS. Any fool finds wisdom foolish. 480

PENTHEUS. Is this the first place you have introduced this god?

DIONYSUS. His rites are danced everywhere abroad.

PENTHEUS. Where they have less control of their senses than us Greeks.

DIONYSUS. Perhaps more. Practices differ.

PENTHEUS. These practices. Do you practise by day or at night?

DIONYSUS. Mainly at night. Devotion needs the dark.

PENTHEUS. So does corrupting women.

DIONYSUS. That can be done in daylight.

PENTHEUS. You'll pay for this disgusting sophistry.

DIONYSUS. And you for your mindless irreverence. 490

PENTHEUS. Is that so? Very brave, this Bacchant, quite a juggler with words.

DIONYSUS. Tell me my fate. What terrible punishment have you in store for me?

PENTHEUS. I shall start by cutting off your curls.

DIONYSUS. My hair is sacred, dressed for the god.

PENTHEUS. Then there's your thyrsus. Hand it over.

DIONYSUS. It belongs to Dionysus. You take it.

PENTHEUS. You we will chain up inside.

DIONYSUS. The god will free me whenever I want.

PENTHEUS. Very fine with your Bacchants all round you.

500   DIONYSUS. Take care. He came with me and sees what I suffer.

PENTHEUS. And where is that then? He is not immediately apparent to my eyes.

DIONYSUS. With me. To a blasphemer, invisible.

PENTHEUS. He mocks me. He mocks Thebes. Tie him up.

DIONYSUS. I give you fair warning. It would be unwise to bind me.

PENTHEUS. We shall soon see who has the power here.

DIONYSUS. You see nothing. What you do, what you are, who you are.

PENTHEUS. That I can tell you. Pentheus, son of Agave and Echion, my father.

DIONYSUS. Pentheus, an ill-omened name. It suits you.

510   PENTHEUS. Take him down. Put him in the stables. He can dance in the dark in there. As for this pack of followers he brought with him, I'll sell them or put them to work sewing instead of making all this din.

DIONYSUS. As you wish. I cannot suffer what I may not. He will repay you for your behaviour, Dionysus, whose existence you deny. When you place a restriction on me, it is Dionysus you affront.

Exeunt DIONYSUS, SERVANT and PENTHEUS.

CHORUS. Dirce, maiden, mistress,
Achelous' daughter,
520   Once you kept Zeus' son
Safe in your spring water.
In his thigh Zeus placed him,
Snatched him from the pyre.
'Enter my male womb,
Safe from deathless fire.'
Bacchios. Dionysus.

530   Dirce, blessed mistress,
Why reject me now?
Why disown my worship,
The garlands on my brow?
Why do you oppress me?
This I swear, one day

You'll accept the worship
Which you now gainsay.
Bromius. Dionysus.

Dragon-seed Pentheus betrays his birth,   540
True son of Echion, sprung from the earth.
Hardly a human, so savage a creature,
God-fighting giant, bloody in feature.
There where our leader lies in the gloom,
Bromius' servants he seeks to entomb.
Do you see from Olympus your witnesses' plight?   550
Come and protect us from tyranny's might.

Where Dionysus? Carrying the thyrsus?
On beast-haunted Nysa, in shade of Olympus?
On crest of Corycia? Where Dionysus?

There he lingers, there he lingers,   560
There where, charming beast in tree-lined glade,
Charming forest, Orpheus played.
You Bromius reveres, blessed Pieria:
Dancing he comes, here he comes prancing,
Never grows weary.   570

From the land of fine horses
Across Axios and Lydia
From the land of fine waters
He hastens, he hastens
Our Maenad leader.
DIONYSUS (*within*). Ahhh, Bacchae. Hear me, Bacchae. Hear my
voice.
CHORUS. Who? Where? A shout. A cry. His. Whose?
Calling. Who?
DIONYSUS (*within*). Hear me, Bacchae. I call again. It is I,   580
Bacchae, son of Semele, son of Zeus.
CHORUS. Dionysus. Master. Dionysus. Join us. Lead us,
Dionysus. Welcome. Bromius, Dionysus.
DIONYSUS (*within*). Come, earthquake, come. Shake the world
to its roots.

127

CHORUS. Help us. Look. Look there. There. The palace of
Pentheus. See, see how it shakes. Shaking to pieces.
It falls. The palace is falling. Dionysus within.
590 Worship him, worship. We revere. We revere. Look
at the stones, the pillars, the beams. Bromius
cries and the whole house replies.

DIONYSUS (*within*). Lightning bolt! Flashing fire! Engulf and
consume all Pentheus' domain.

CHORUS. See how it blazes. Blazing fire licking over the
holy tomb. Over Semele's tomb, Semele blasted by
thunderbolt, thunderbolt of Zeus. Fling yourself
600 earthwards, fling yourself fearfully. Cast down
your bodies. Fall down you Maenads. All-overturning,
Zeus' child breaks the house down.
Enter DIONYSUS.

DIONYSUS. Women, outsiders. Were you so terror-stricken you
fell to the ground? I do believe you may have noticed how
Dionysus wobbled the palace of Pentheus. Up you get. Calm
yourselves. There, that's better.

CHORUS. Light of our light, lord of our Bacchic rites,
we are overjoyed to see you, we have been so desolate.

610 DIONYSUS. You lost all heart, did you, believing I had fallen
into one of Pentheus' dark traps?

CHORUS. How could we help it? What protection was left us?
But how are you free from that vile man's authority?

DIONYSUS. Saving myself was really no problem.

CHORUS. Your hands were tied, bound up with chains.

DIONYSUS. I made a fool of him. He thought that he had tied
me up, but he never touched me. Delusion. By the stable
when he thought he was securing me, he trussed up a bull,
620 shin and hoof. But it was he who snorted all the while, and
gnawed his lips, sweat pouring off him, and I stood quietly
by, surveying the scene. Then came Dionysus to burn up
house and tomb. When the King saw that he ran about telling
servants to fetch water. They were all too busy, slaving away
. . . to no avail I need hardly add. Then he changed tack.
Deciding that I had escaped, he grabbed a sword and rushed
indoors. Then Dionysus, or so I suppose – it is only what I

assume happened – fashioned a phantom inside the house.
Pentheus made straight for it, this ethereal shining thing,   630
thinking to kill me. Then Dionysus mocked him even more.
He razed the house to the ground. Turned it upside down.
That will teach him to tie me up. Pentheus dropped his sword
when he saw that. A man daring to take on a god. Imagine!
As for me I simply slipped out here to you. Pentheus is
nothing. I think I hear him coming. What will he have to say,
I wonder. Not that his bluster upsets me greatly. Controlling
one's temper is the sign of a wise man.   640

Enter PENTHEUS.

PENTHEUS. This is humiliating. That foreigner, chained as he
  was a minute ago, he's got away. So the fellow's here, is he?
  What is all this? How did you get out? What do you think
  you are doing standing here in front of my house?
DIONYSUS. Don't take it too hard. And don't come any closer.
PENTHEUS. How did you get out?
DIONYSUS. Did I not tell you that someone would free me.
  Perhaps you were not listening.
PENTHEUS. Someone? What someone? Give a straight answer,
  can't you?   650
DIONYSUS. The god who grew the clustering vine for man.
DIONYSUS. That, I suppose, is a Dionysiac benefit.
DIONYSUS. His presence here you can bear witness to.
PENTHEUS. I'll have every gate in the the walls bolted.
DIONYSUS. To what end? Cannot a god jump over a wall?
PENTHEUS. You're clever, so clever. But not as clever as all that.
DIONYSUS. As all that especially, because I was born wise.
  Perhaps you should pay attention to what this messenger of
  yours has to say. Don't worry. I will not run away.
  Enter FIRST MESSENGER.
MESSENGER. Pentheus, Lord of Thebes, I come from Cithaeron   660
  where the snow can fall so thick and white . . .
PENTHEUS. Do you have any news or don't you?
MESSENGER. Bacchants. That is what I have seen, rushing about
  like mad things. Barefoot. All over the place. I tell you, my

129

lord, these things they get up to, they're amazing. More than
amazing. Do you want me to tell you everything? Or give you
670 an edited version? To tell the truth, my lord, I'm a bit
apprehensive about how you'll take it.

PENTHEUS. Tell me it all. You'll come to no harm from me. I
have no need to take out my temper on decent people. The
worse the tale you have to tell about these Bacchants, the
more severe my punishment for their corruption will be.

MESSENGER. It was soon after daybreak, the sun just getting
680 warm. My cattle were heading for the tops when I saw them,
three groups of these dancing women. Autonoe was the leader
of one group, your mother Agave the second, Ino the third.
They were all fast asleep, stretched out, some reclining on pine
branches, others amongst the oak leaves. They were lying
anywhere, but decently: no sign of the drink and music you
had told us about, no dissipation in the bushes. Then your
mother, when she heard my cattle lowing, gave a great shout,
690 and jumped up in the middle of the others crying, 'Rouse your
bodies from sleep.' And they all threw off their sleepiness and
stood upright, old and young, married and unmarried, a
marvellous sight. They let down their hair, tied up their
fawnskins where they had become disarranged, and hung on
their dappled fur snakes which licked their cheeks. Some
young ones with milk at the breast, their newborn children
700 deserted, nursed gazelles or fed young cubs. Then they dressed
their hair with ivy, oak or flowered briony. One struck her
thyrsus on a rock and a stream of water flowed out. Another
710 planted hers in the ground and it sprayed out god-given wine.
Those who required milk had only to scratch in the earth for it
to pour out. Their ivy wands were dripping with honey. I tell
you, had you been there and seen all this, you would be
praying to the god you now pour scorn upon. We got together,
herdsmen and shepherds, arguing about all these wonderful
things. Some clever fellow, no countryman, made an
720 announcement. 'How about it, men of the hills? Shall we hunt
down Agave, the king's mother, out of these revels, and do our
lord a favour?' It seemed like a good idea, so we laid an
ambush in the brush and waited. In a short while, they all

started shaking their wands and shouting to Iacchus, calling on
Bromius, son of Zeus. The whole mountain went wild for
Dionysus, animals too. They began to run. Everything ran.
Agave came leaping past where I was hiding. I tried to grab
her, but she let out a scream. 'Hounds, my swift hounds. They   730
are hunting us. Men. Arm with your thyrsi. Arm. Follow me.'
And we fled. They'd have torn us to pieces, these Bacchants.
They turned instead on our herds where they were feeding.

   With her bare hands your own mother wrenched and tore
at a bellowing cow. Others ripped at calves, stripping them.   740
Hooves torn off. Ribs wherever you looked. Pieces of flesh,
hanging bloody from the trees, dripping. Even bulls, with
pride of horn, were dragged down, set upon by dozens of
girlish hands, which grabbed at them, defleshing them as
quickly as you could wink, my lord. Then off they sprinted,
swift as birds, down to the fertile Theban plain, to Hysia and 750
Erythrae beneath Cithaeron. Like enemies they invaded,
scattering everything. They snatched children out of houses,
slung them over their shoulders where they stuck fast, as did
anything they carried, even iron and steel, nothing falling to
earth. They bore fire in their hair. It didn't even scorch them.
The villagers, meanwhile, furious at the raid, fell to arms, but
there's another mystery, my lord. The steel javelins of the   760
villagers didn't so much as draw blood, but the thyrsi cast by
the Bacchants wounded them and put them to flight. Men,
routed by women, but not without the help of a god. Then
they went back where they'd come from, to the fountains the
god had raised up for them. They washed off the blood, while
the snakes licked clean their cheeks. This god, my lord,
whoever he is, accept him in the city. His power is   770
phenomenal, greater even than I have told you. He is the one,
as they say, who gives mankind wine to sooth his ills. And
without wine, there's no love either, and not too much else for
a man to enjoy.
CHORUS. I hesitated to speak of freedom before such a tyrant,
   but speak I must. Second to no god is our god
   Dionysus.
PENTHEUS. It is upon us already, spreading like wildfire, this

Bacchanalian frenzy. The whole of Greece will be jeering at
780   us. We must act. You, go to the Electran gate. I want the
shield-carriers, the cavalry and bowmen. Fast riders, the best
shots. We march against the Bacchae. It is past all enduring
to put up with these women's conduct.

DIONYSUS. Pentheus, you take no notice of what I say. I have
suffered at your hands, but I am giving you fair warning. Do
790   not bear arms against a god. Calm down. Dionysus will never
allow you to drive his followers from the mountains.

PENTHEUS. Don't give me orders. You are free. Isn't that
enough? Or are you looking for further punishment?

DIONYSUS. It seems to me you would do better to offer him a
sacrifice, rather than get so excited. You cannot fight against
the inevitable, mortal against immortal.

PENTHEUS. I'll offer a sacrifice all right . . . all those women. In
the woods on Cithaeron they'll get the sacrifice they deserve.

DIONYSUS. You will simply run away, even with metal shields
against wooden thyrsi. And you will all look rather foolish.

800   PENTHEUS. I have had enough of this foreigner. Nothing I do or
say will stop his mouth.

DIONYSUS. My good sir, listen to me. This could still be turned
to your advantage.

PENTHEUS. What can I do? I cannot let my subjects overrule
me, women at that.

DIONYSUS. I will bring the women back. Unharmed.

PENTHEUS. Indeed. You are plotting something.

DIONYSUS. Why should I be plotting anything, beyond using my
skill to assist you?

PENTHEUS. You are in this together, plotting to install this
religion here.

DIONYSUS. Why yes, I am. I am in this together with a god.

PENTHEUS. That's enough from you. Fetch me my armour.

DIONYSUS. One thing more. You would like to watch them up
810   there in the mountains, would you not?

PENTHEUS. Watch them? Why yes. I would pay good money to
see what they are up to.

DIONYSUS. Why this great desire to see them?

PENTHEUS. There's no great pleasure in watching women drunk.

132

DIONYSUS. But you would like to take a look, pleasant sight or not.

PENTHEUS. Yes I would. As long as I was sitting quietly out of the way among the trees.

DIONYSUS. They would sniff you out if you tried to be furtive about it.

PENTHEUS. That's very true. Out in the open then.

DIONYSUS. Do you want me to show you a way? Is that what you want?

PENTHEUS. Yes. You show me the way. Now. I want to go now. 820

DIONYSUS. You will have to put on a dress. Linen, something like that.

PENTHEUS. A dress? What do you mean? Dress like a woman?

DIONYSUS. They would murder a man if they saw him, now wouldn't they?

PENTHEUS. Yes, of course. You are right. You have thought it all out.

DIONYSUS. Call it inspiration. From Dionysus.

PENTHEUS. A clever idea. Now what?

DIONYSUS. Come indoors. I will help get you dressed.

PENTHEUS. Get dressed. I don't think I have the nerve. Not like a woman.

DIONYSUS. Do you want a peep at the Maenads, or do you not?

PENTHEUS. A dress, you say? What sort of a dress do you have in mind for me? 830

DIONYSUS. The dress should be full length. And a wig, a long one.

PENTHEUS. Any other kind of decoration?

DIONYSUS. You ought to have a headband.

PENTHEUS. Is that everything?

DIONYSUS. Yes, except for a thyrsus and fawnskin.

PENTHEUS. I couldn't do it. I couldn't dress up like a woman.

DIONYSUS. The alternative is bloodshed and a battle against the Bacchae.

PENTHEUS. All right. I'll do it. I really must get a look at them before anything else.

DIONYSUS. Far more sensible than countering one evil with another.

840 PENTHEUS. How will I cross the city without being recognised?

DIONYSUS. We'll use quiet roads. I'll take you.

PENTHEUS. Anything is better than having those Bacchants
laugh at me. I'll go inside. I want to think about it.

DIONYSUS. As you wish. I am prepared whatever you decide.

PENTHEUS. I'll go then. I will go and prepare my weapons.
Either that, or do what you suggest.

Exit PENTHEUS.

DIONYSUS. Straight into the trap. Where he will find, oh my
women, his Bacchants and his death warrant. Dionysus, close
at hand, now it is up to you. We will pay him out, but first
befuddle his wits, make him mad. Never in his right mind

850 would he put on a dress. Possessed, he will. After all those
dire threats of his, I want Thebes helpless with laughter as he
primps, ladylike, through the streets. I will go and help him
into the shroud he must wear when his mother tears him

860 apart. He will discover, at first hand, Dionysus, son of Zeus,
most fearful of gods by nature, though the mildest too.

Exit DIONYSUS.

CHORUS. I long to dance through the night without sleeping,
Barefoot,
Neck stretched up to the dew-dropping air,
Like a fawn as she plays in the field,
Fear flown,
Flight-free,
Escaped from the huntsman's snare,

870 Where she strained as she strove as she ran,
Past meadow,
Past stream,
Till she found forest peace, far from man.

Where is the beginning of wisdom?
What gift of the gods could be finer for man
Than to raise up his hand o'er the head of his foe,

880 Triumphant.
Nothing finer,
Delightful.

The power of the gods proceeds slowly but surely,
Chastening
The insensitive,
Those whose mad arrogance trusts only itself.
Hidden away lie the traps for the godless.
Time passes,
Slowfoot.
The gods have good time to await the unwary.　　　　　890
We must know and must care for the custom of ages,
What's right and what's natural.
These the ideals that religion gives sanction to.

Where is the beginning of wisdom?
What gift of the gods could be finer for man
Than to raise up his hand o'er the head of his foe,
Triumphant.　　　　　900
Nothing finer.
Delightful.

Happy the man who escapes the sea's tempest.
Peace,
A haven he finds
Delivered from hardship.
One achieves one thing, another another,
Fortune and happiness,
Hope upon hope.
So to thousands of men may be myriad ambitions.
Some may achieve while others fall backward.
Happy the man who can daily progress.　　　　　910
Enter DIONYSUS.

DIONYSUS. Pentheus, so keen to see what you ought not to see,
　　come out, Pentheus, out from your palace. Let's have a look
　　at you, tricked out like a Bacchant to go and spy on your
　　mother and her troupe.
　　Enter PENTHEUS.
　　There now, every inch a daughter of Cadmus.

PENTHEUS. I can see two suns, I think, and the seven-gated
　　city, Thebes, double. A bull. You appear before me as a bull.　　920

135

Horns on your head? A wild animal. Did you used to be an
animal? You have become a bull.

DIONYSUS. The god is with us. He was ill-disposed before, but
now he has joined us. You are seeing as you ought to see.

PENTHEUS. Who do I look like? Ino, surely, though perhaps
more like my mother, Agave?

DIONYSUS. Their living image. You could be either one. Wait.
A lock of hair is out of place. Tuck it back in the hood where
I set it.

930 PENTHEUS. I must have loosened it when I was shaking my head
about, Bacchant-fashion.

DIONYSUS. Let me be your dresser. Keep your head still. There.

PENTHEUS. Set me to rights. I am in your hands now.

DIONYSUS. The girdle could be tighter, and your dress is not
hanging quite right at the ankle.

PENTHEUS. I see. On the right. The left is all right though, isn't
it?

940 DIONYSUS. How you will thank me when you finally see the
Bacchants and find out that you are wrong about them.

PENTHEUS. What is the right way to hold a thyrsus? This hand,
is it? I want to be like a real Bacchant.

DIONYSUS. Right hand, and you raise your right foot in time.
Good, that's it. I do commend this change of heart.

PENTHEUS. I wonder if I could lift up Cithaeron on my
shoulders, and all the Bacchae with it.

DIONYSUS. Anything you like. Your wits were distracted before.
Now they are sound again.

PENTHEUS. What about taking a crowbar? Or shall I just put a
shoulder against the cliffs and heave them over, with brute
950 force?

DIONYSUS. You do not want to do any harm to the holy places
of the nymphs, now do you, or the haunts of Pan, which echo
with his pipes?

PENTHEUS. No, of course. And it would not be right to use
force against a woman. I will hide in the trees.

DIONYSUS. You will find the right hiding-place for someone who
wants to peer at the Bacchae.

PENTHEUS. I think I can see them already in the bushes, at it like sparrows.

DIONYSUS. That is why you are going – as a watchdog. Perhaps 960
you will catch them. Unless they catch you first.

PENTHEUS. Take me through the centre of Thebes as I am the
only man with the nerve to go.

DIONYSUS. You bear responsibility for Thebes, all by yourself.
You alone. Your trial awaits. Follow me. I will deliver you
safely. Someone else can return you.

PENTHEUS. My mother.

DIONYSUS. For everyone to see.

PENTHEUS. That is why I am going.

DIONYSUS. You will be carried back . . .

PENTHEUS. In triumph.

DIONYSUS. In your mother's arms.

PENTHEUS. You will ruin me.

DIONYSUS. You could say that.

PENTHEUS. Not that I don't deserve it. 970

Exit PENTHEUS.

DIONYSUS. What a remarkable man you are, but you face an
ordeal so remarkable it will bring you fame in heaven. Such
an ordeal and so young a man. But I will win. You will see.
Bromius and I will win.

Exit DIONYSUS.

CHORUS. Go. Swift. Hounds. Madness.
Sting. Madness. Sting.
Cadmus' daughters,
Madness, sting. 980
Maenad spy decked out as female.

Mother spies. Spy from rock or spy from tree.
'Spy, Bacchae, racing Bacchae.'
Spy's mother. 'No, women.
Lioncub. Gorgon-spawn.' 990

Sword of Justice, sword through throat
Of the godless, lawless, worthless man.

Echion's son, stung with madness,

Fighting your mysteries, Dionysus.
1000   And his mother's. Fights from weakness,
Crazed with daring, fighting mysteries.

Carefree life? Behave like mortals.
Cleverness for the clever. I choose better.
Reverence, honour, respect for the gods,
These man should practise by day and by night.

1010   Sword of Justice, sword through throat
Of the godless, lawless, worthless man.

Come, Dionysus, appear as a bull,
As a many-mouthed dragon,
As fire-breathing lion.

1020   Come, Bacchios. Come Bacchios.
Hunt, mock, trap, Bacchios.
Pursue him, sneer at him, snare him,
The man who would chase your Maenads.
Collapsed at their feet
He will find what he looked for.
Enter SECOND MESSENGER.

MESSENGER. Nothing but grief. I'm only a slave but I grieve for
   my masters, as a good slave must. This family, till now so
   prosperous throughout Greece, family of Cadmus, the dragon-
   seed sower . . . grief . . .

CHORUS. Tell us. What news of the Bacchae?

1030 MESSENGER. The son of Echion, Pentheus. Dead.

CHORUS. Dionysus, Lord, you show your true face. Great
   is the god Dionysus.

MESSENGER. What? What are you saying, woman? You rejoice
   at this family's disaster?

CHORUS. No family of mine. I am free to sing my foreign songs,
   safe from the fear of restraint.

MESSENGER. Thebes has men enough . . .

CHORUS. Dionysus is my master. Not Thebes. Dionysus.

MESSENGER. Maybe so, but even you should not rejoice at such terrible things. It cannot be right. 1040

CHORUS. Tell me. The whole story. How did he die, this
evil worker of evil deeds?

MESSENGER. We left the last cottages of Thebes behind, and
crossed the Asopus heading for Cithaeron. Just Pentheus,
myself in attendance and that foreigner to show us the way. As
soon as we got there we sank down in a grassy hollow to
watch, silent and unseen. There's a rift between tall cliffs, 1050
waterfalls running down them, all shaded by pine trees. That's
where we saw the Maenads, hard at work, but content. Some
were decorating thyrsi with sprigs of new ivy. Others sung
Bacchic songs to one another, frisking about, free as colts.
Pentheus could not see the whole band of them and he said,
poor man, 'I cannot view these self-styled Maenads properly 1060
from here. If I could climb up higher, in one of those pines
perhaps, I could get a better look at this debauchery of theirs.'
Then I saw the foreigner do an extraordinary thing. He took
hold of a soaring branch from one of the pines, and he pulled
it, pulled it right down to the dark earth. He bent it over like
a bow or the curved felloe on a wheel. Just so did this strange
man take that tree in his two hands, and bend it to the
ground. No ordinary man could have done it. His strength was
superhuman. He sat Pentheus astride the branches, and let the 1070
tree slowly straighten, taking care not to unseat him. Up it
went, up towards the sky, my master on its back, for all the
Maenads to see, plainer than he saw them. No sooner was
Pentheus up there in full view than the foreigner disappeared
and a voice came out of the air, as it were the voice of
Dionysus. 'Ladies,' he cried, 'he is the man who would make
mock of us and our mysteries. I offer him to you for 1080
punishment.' He spoke and a blinding flash of fire struck earth
from heaven. Everything went quite still, air, trees, animals
even, quite still. The Maenads got to their feet, some having
missed his words, and stared about them. He called again.
This time Cadmus' daughters realised what he required. And
they ran. They ran, swift as birds, Agave, her sisters, all of 1090
them, over river and rock, mad, for the god had breathed on
them. Then they saw my master perched in his tree. They

hurled stones at first and sticks, climbing the cliff opposite.
1100 Some threw thyrsi at their wretched target. He was too high
even for their frenzy, but could only sit there appalled. They
snatched off branches from the oaks to lever up his pine, but
their efforts bore no fruit. Then Agave spoke. 'Circle the
trunk, Maenads, grasp it. We need to catch this clamberer
before he reveals god's dances.' Dozens of hands hauled at the
1110 tree, then heaved it out of the earth. Down fell Pentheus,
down to the ground with an awful cry. He knew now what was
happening. His mother started it, the ritual slaughter.
Desperate Agave. As she fell upon him, he tore off the
headdress so she would recognise him and grabbed her cheek.
'Mother. It is me. It's Pentheus, your son. Pity me. I have
1120 done wrong. Do not kill me.' But her eyes were rolling. She
was frothing, imagining god knows what in her Dionysiac
frenzy. She ignored his words, and took his left hand in hers,
planted a foot in his ribs and tore off his arm at the shoulder.
Her strength was supernatural. Ino set to work on the other
side, tearing out handfuls of flesh, and Autonoe and the whole
1130 mob of Bacchants. A single ghastly scream, Pentheus' agony
and their exultation. One took away an arm, another a foot still
in its shoe. His ribs were stripped to the bone. Bright red
hands toyed with lumps of his flesh. The remains are all over,
by the rocks, in the undergrowth, anywhere. We'll never find
them. But the head, the poor head, his mother chanced to
1140 snatch up, and she stuck it on her thyrsus. She left her sisters
dancing away and set off through Cithaeron, brandishing the
head as though it were a mountain lion's. She arrived in the
city glorying in her frightful trophy, shrieking about her
splendid Dionysus, fellow-huntsman, victorious. A victory of
tears. I cannot stay to see this sight, not Agave's homecoming.
All that people like us can do is think clearly and honour the
1150 gods. That is the only sensible course for mortal man to
follow.
Exit MESSENGER.

CHORUS. Dionysus, we dance for you,
  Call on your name, Dionysus.
  Dionysus, we praise you.

140

Defeat for the dragon-born,
Dragon-spawn Pentheus,
Dressed like a woman,
Clasping a thyrsus,
Passport to Hades,
Led by the bull-god, Dionysus.

Such a famous victory have you achieved,   1160
Bacchants of Cadmus,
A victory for suffering,
A victory for tears.
Fine victory for a mother,
Paddling in her own child's blood.

And here I see her, the mother of Pentheus,
wild-eyed Agave. Welcome to our revelling company.
Enter AGAVE.

AGAVE. Bacchae from Asia.

CHORUS. You call? Ahhh.

AGAVE. See what I have brought home from the mountains. The   1170
garlands are quite fresh. Happy hunting.

CHORUS. I see you and welcome you, my fellow-reveller.

AGAVE. Look. Here is my lion cub, caught without trap.

CHORUS. Where did you find it?

AGAVE. On Cithaeron.

CHORUS. Cithaeron?

AGAVE. Cithaeron killed him.

CHORUS. Who was the first to . . .

AGAVE. I was. Fortunate Agave. That's what they are calling   1180
me.

CHORUS. Any others?

AGAVE. Cadmus' daughters.

CHORUS. Cadmus'?

AGAVE. They fingered the prey. But after me, after me. Good
luck in the hunt. Will you share the feast with me?

CHORUS. Share, poor woman, share?

AGAVE. It is just a cub. Soft mane and downy whiskers.

CHORUS. Mane, yes, and whiskers,

1190   AGAVE. It was a clever hunter, Dionysus himself, who set us on
        to our prey.

        CHORUS. Our lord, the hunter.

        AGAVE. Have I done well?

        CHORUS. Of course. Very well.

        AGAVE. Soon all the men in Thebes . . .

        CHORUS. And Pentheus, your son Pentheus.

        AGAVE. Oh, he will be pleased with his mother for capturing
        such a lion-cub.

        CHORUS. A rare prize.

        AGAVE. Rare is right.

        CHORUS. Are you pleased?

        AGAVE. Ecstatically so. Anyone can see what a fine creature I
        have bagged.

1200   CHORUS. Show it then. Show everyone this trophy, poor
        woman, this trophy you bring.

        AGAVE. Citizens of our dear Thebes, draw near and examine the
        spoil. We, Cadmus' daughters, have captured it without spear
        or net. With just our white fingers. So much for the boasting
        of men and their weaponry. This creature we dissected with
1210   our bare hands. Where's my old father? Send for him. And
        Pentheus. Where's my son Pentheus? He can climb up with
        this lion's head and nail it over the door.

        Enter CADMUS attended.

        CADMUS. Follow me in. Bring him here, here in front of his
        own house – what is left of him. Poor Pentheus. I found his
        body spread over Cithaeron, all torn, in pieces. I found
1220   something in the wood . . . I was on the way back from
        revelling with old Teiresias when they told me what my
        daughers had done. I went back to the mountain and found
        the boy. The Bacchae had . . . killed him. Actaeon's mother,
        Autonoe, was there. Ino too, in among the oak groves, still
        raving. But someone told me that Agave has wandered back
1230   here in her mania. How right they were, I cannot look.

        AGAVE. Father. Now you can be proud of us. What daughters
        you have sired, the best in all the world. And especially me.
        I've left my weaving behind and gone on to hunting, and with
        my bare hands. Look here. No, what I am holding in my

142

arms, a trophy to mount on the palace walls. Here take hold
of it, father, and let's call our friends to a celebration. They'll   1240
think well of you for this.

CADMUS. No man could measure the horror of what I see.
Murder, vile murder at those frightful hands. This is the
victim you want Thebes to celebrate. My grief is for you. For
me too. A just revenge? No, too cruel. Dionysus is one of our
family, but he has destroyed our house.   1250

AGAVE. How cross an old man can get. Looking at me like that.
I want my son to take after his mother, racing to the hunt
with the young men of Thebes. All he does is fight gods. You
should put him right, father. It's your place. Call him here,
someone, so he can see how well I have done.

CADMUS. Oh my dear. When you realise what you have done,
your pain will be unbearable. Stark madness is the best you   1260
can hope for.

AGAVE. What's gone wrong? Why so solemn?

CADMUS. Look up. Look at the sky.

AGAVE. Very well. What am I meant to be looking at?

CADMUS. Is it the same as before, or do you see a change?

AGAVE. It's brighter, perhaps, a little clearer.

CADMUS. And the confusion in your mind. Is that still with you?

AGAVE. I don't understand. I was confused, but that seems to be   1270
passing.

CADMUS. Can you hear what I am saying? Tell me if you can.

AGAVE. What were we just talking about? Father, I can't
remember

CADMUS. What family was it you married into?

AGAVE. You gave me to Echion, the one they called the dragon-
spawn.

CADMUS. Yes, and the son you bore your husband?

AGAVE. Pentheus. Our son is Pentheus.

CADMUS. And whose . . . whose head is that you are cradling in
your arms?

AGAVE. A lion's. That's what the hunters told me.

CADMUS. Look at it. No fully. Just a look.

AGAVE. What is it? What am I holding?   1280

CADMUS. Look again. Carefully. Now do you realise?

AGAVE. What I see is unbearable. God help me.

CADMUS. Is it anything like a lion?

AGAVE. God help me. The head is Pentheus.

CADMUS. We wept. We knew. You never realised.

AGAVE. Who killed him? Why am I carrying this?

CADMUS. Best not to know. The truth is terrible.

AGAVE. Tell me. My heart is pounding, I have to know.

CADMUS. You killed him. And your sisters. You killed him.

1290 AGAVE. Where? at home? Somewhere else?

CADMUS. There where his own hounds ripped Actaeon to pieces.

AGAVE. Whatever was the poor boy doing on Cithaeron?

CADMUS. He went to make fun of your Dionysus and his rites.

AGAVE. Our Dionysus? What were we doing there?

CADMUS. You did not know what you were doing. The whole
city was deranged.

AGAVE. Now I see it. Dionysus has destroyed us.

CADMUS. He was slighted. You slighted him by refusing to
believe in his divinity.

AGAVE. Where is my son's body, father?

CADMUS. There are the remains. It wasn't easy . . .

1300 AGAVE. The body is . . . all there?

CADMUS. Don't look. The head you have. That is what I could
find.

AGAVE. How did Pentheus get involved in this madness of
mine?

CADMUS. Like you he disdained the god. We are all involved in
this disaster, you, the son you see here dead, and me as well.
No male heirs. The family is destroyed. This house looked up
to you, my boy. My grandson, my support. They went in awe

1310 of you in Thebes. No one could insult the old man when you
were around. Or else you made him pay. Dishonoured I must
leave my home, Cadmus the great, founder of Thebes, sower
and reaper of the finest of races. I loved you most. In death I
love you still. Never again to hug you, to feel your touch on
my cheek, or hear your voice: 'Is something the matter,

1320 grandfather? Is someone upsetting you? Tell me. I'll soon put
a stop to it.' Now I am desolate, and so are you. Mother,
daughters, pitiful. If any here cast doubt on supernatural

144

power, let him consider this boy's death, and take heed.
CHORUS. Cadmus, you have my pity. Your daughter's child, he
got what he deserved, but the pain is yours.
AGAVE. Father, you see the change in me . . . [*The manuscript
breaks off here.*]
Conjectural reconstruction.

Same now, I see what I could not see. My own child,
Pentheus. How did I not know him? My sisters too? My son's
blood is upon these hands, loving hands which tore away his
life. And I am left to mourn the son who should have mourned
for me. Whose fate is worse? Here place the head and cover it.
Cover it quickly. Dionysus was the cause and now I know his
power. What mortal man could stand and face his fury?
Enter DIONYSUS above.

DIONYSUS. What mortal man indeed? I am Dionysus, son of
Zeus and of your sister Semele. I came to Thebes to seek my
earthly home. But how was I received? The city rejected me.
My family cast me out, me, a god, they banished from their
mortal company. My mother Semele's sisters I drove mad up
into the mountains, and they have done what I had them do.
So all of you as exiles must seek your own redemption, an
expiation which only time can bring. Pentheus, my cousin,
who dared to sneer at my rites, I mocked in my turn, and sent
him Bacchios – mad to where his mother was waiting.

Lacuna ends.

For Cadmus, my grandfather, and Harmonia his wife, a   1330
different fate is in store. You shall turn into snakes – Zeus'
oracle has forecast this – and lead great armies. Strange deeds
and in strange places, with no peace at the last. Leading
barbarian hordes, you will sack cities and even Apollo's oracle,
though that will bring a grim return. But Ares, Harmonia's
father, will preserve you and take you eventually to the land of
the Blessed. That is my immortal decree, and I am the son of
Zeus, Dionysus, a good friend to the wise. A pity you did not   1340
realise it sooner.

CADMUS. Dionysus, we implore you. We admit that we were
  wrong.

DIONYSUS. Too late. You acknowledge me far too late.

CADMUS. We know that, but you are too severe.

DIONYSUS. You offended me, me a god.

CADMUS. A god should not show passion like a man.

DIONYSUS. Zeus assented to all this long ago.

1350 AGAVE. Come now, father, exile is our fate.

DIONYSUS. Go then. Why put off the inevitable?

CADMUS. We have come to a terrible pass, my child, every one
  of us, your sisters too. An old man I must go and live in
  foreign lands, fated, with Harmonia, my wife, daughter of
  Ares, to lead an alien army against Greece: changed to a snake,
  but warlord against the altars and tombs of my country. No
  peace for me until I cross Acheron's stream.

1360 AGAVE. I must go too, father, and I must part from you.

CADMUS. Why cling to me, poor child, like a young white swan
  still clinging to an old?

AGAVE. Where can I turn, cast out from my country?

CADMUS. I do not know, my dear. Your father cannot help you.

AGAVE. Farewell. Home, city, country. An exile.

1370 CADMUS. Go to Aristaeus. He will protect you

AGAVE. Father, I feel pity for you.

CADMUS. And I for you. Your sisters too.

AGAVE. This punishment Dionysus has visited on our family. It
  is terrible.

DIONYSUS. What you made me suffer was terrible, my name
  disparaged in Thebes.

AGAVE. Father. Farewell.

1380 CADMUS. Farewell, my child. Though what can fare well mean?

AGAVE. Take me to my sisters, my poor fellow-exiles. I want to
  go where cursed Cithaeron shall never see me more, nor I set
  eyes on Cithaeron. Some place where I can forget the thyrsus.
  All that I leave to others.

  Exeunt AGAVE and CADMUS.

CHORUS. However clear they may appear,
  The gods are seldom what they seem.

1390   The unexpected is the theme

Of the mystery acted here.

Exit CHORUS.

A Note on the Translators

JEREMY BROOKS is the author of four novels, three screenplays, many television and radio plays and two stage plays. His English stage adaptations include six plays by Maxim Gorky, others by Gogol, Chekhov, Tolstoy, Ostrovsky, Solzhenitsyn, Ibsen, Strindberg, Brecht and, with Adrian Mitchell, Dylan Thomas's *A Child's Christmas in Wales*. He was Literary Manager for the Royal Shakespeare Company and Literary Adviser for Theatre Toronto. He is currently an Artistic Associate at Theatr Clwyd. Brought up in Llandudno, he has had a home in Llanfrothen, Meirioneth, since 1983. His most recent publication is *Doing the Voices*, four novellas.

DAVID THOMPSON, whose main career as an art critic has included seven years writing for *The Times*, a number of award-winning art films, television programmes and a biography of Raphael, directed his first Greek tragedy, *The Bacchae*, when reading Classics at Oxford. With his own company, Stage Sixty, he mounted a two-month Euripides season at the Theatre Royal, Stratford East, in 1964, consisting of *Electra*, *The Trojan Women* and *Iphigeneia in Tauris*, and has also directed *The Bacchae* at the Edinburgh Festival and *Medea* and *The Phoenician Women* (retitled *The Sons of Oedipus*) at the Greenwich Theatre. His translations include *Electra*, Aeschylus' *Prometheus Bound* (both of which, together with *The Sons of Oedipus*, have been broadcast), *Medea* and Sophocles' *Oedipus at Colonus*, as well as three plays by Molière.

J. MICHAEL WALTON worked in the professional theatre as an actor and director before joining the University of Hull, where he is Reader in Theatre History in the Drama Department. He has published three books on Greek theatre, *Greek Theatre Practice*, *The Greek Sense of Theatre: Tragedy Reviewed*, and *Living Greek Theatre: A Handbook of Classical Performance and Modern Production*. He has also published in a number of areas of more modern British and European theatre, is the editor of *Craig on Theatre* and General Editor of Methuen Classical Drama in Translation.

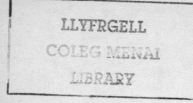